other books by jeanne safer

Beyond Motherhood: *Choosing a Life without Children*

Forgiving and Not Forgiving: *A New Approach to Resolving*
Intimate Betrayal

for judith kaufman

Jeanne Safer, Ph.D.

The Free Press New York London Toronto Sydney Singapore

The

Normal

One

Life with a Difficult or Damaged Sibling

THE FREE PRESS
A Division of Simon & Schuster, Inc.
1230 Avenue of the Americas
New York, NY 10020

THE FREE PRESS and colophon are trademarks
of Simon & Schuster, Inc.

Designed by Bonni Leon-Berman

Manufactured in the United States of America

10   9   8   7   6   5   4   3   2   1

Library of Congress Cataloging-in-Publication Data
Safer, Jeanne.
      The normal one : life with a difficult or damaged sibling / Jeanne Safer.
         p.   cm.
      Includes bibiliographical references and index.
      1. Brothers and sisters.   2. Problem children—Family relationships.   I. Title.

      BF723.S43 .S13 2002
      158.2'4—dc21

                                                                              2002067529
ISBN 0-7432-1196-0

For information regarding special discounts for bulk purchases,
please contact Simon & Schuster Special Sales at 1-800-456-6798
or business@simonandschuster.com

author's note

The names and identifying characteristics of everyone interviewed in this book have been changed.

acknowledgments

I WANT TO THANK the "normal ones" I interviewed for their generosity, courage, and insight; I hope I did justice to their experience. Don Meyer, founder of Sibnet, and the siblings who participate in this invaluable Internet network welcomed me. My research assistant Marcey Needel was of immense help and relentless in her pursuit of every possible document on this elusive subject. I am indebted to my editor, Philip Rappaport, and my agent, Jennifer Rudolph Walsh, for believing in my work and for giving me the opportunity to write this book. Special gratitude goes to my dear friends Sue Grand, Leonard Schoolman, and Harriet Wald for their encouragement; to Paul Russo for assistance both technical and emotional; and to my husband Richard Brookhiser for sustaining me. *The Normal One* is dedicated to my beloved friend and colleague Judith Kaufman, whose observation years ago I never forgot: "Someday you will have to write about your brother."

I traveled around a great deal . . . I would have stopped, but I was pursued by something. It always came upon me unawares . . . Then all at once my sister touched my shoulder. I turn around and look into her eyes. Oh Laura, Laura, I tried to leave you behind me, but I am more faithful than I intended to be!

The Glass Menagerie by Tennessee Williams

contents

introduction

NOBODY KNOWS I HAVE A BROTHER. My best friends never hear his name. He has always been a source of embarrassment and discomfort for me, but I've never wondered very much about his impact on my life. Being his sister feels vaguely unreal and irrelevant; my destiny has nothing to do with his.

This is astonishing, because I am a psychotherapist who has spent years trying to understand my own and my patients' childhoods. Somehow I've managed to erase my own closest relative.

I am not alone. Beyond slogans ("all men are brothers," "sisterhood is powerful") and the occasional soft-focus picture book, shockingly little attention is paid to siblings in general, much less to troubled, difficult, or disabled ones. And although millions of people have such relatives—85 percent of Americans have siblings, so few extended families are exempt—practically nothing has been written about them. Worse, little has been *thought* about them; newspaper headlines (the Kaczynski brothers, wayward presidential siblings), literature (Dostoyevsky's *The Brothers Karamazov*, the plays of Williams and O'Neill), the Bible (Cain and Abel, Joseph and his brothers), and the dreams of their higher-functioning brothers and sisters tell their story, not psychological research.

Their influence is intensified because it is so hidden, even in a culture where people willingly expose the most intimate details of their lives.

The purpose of this book is to reveal the neglected, lonely, and lifelong trauma of growing up with an abnormal brother or sister and its effects on personality and society; the reality of the lives of the "normal ones" is far more complex than the sentimental image presented by the media and even by their own families. It examines the world all such siblings share, whether the disability is mental or physical, minor or catastrophic, ignored or overemphasized. It analyzes how and why their influence is repudiated, and offers remedies.

Normal ones suffer from a psychological condition I name "the Caliban Syndrome" after the brutal, repugnant slave of the magician Prospero in Shakespeare's *The Tempest*, the not-quite-human creature who tried to rape Prospero's flawless daughter Miranda. Caliban is the "thing of darkness" Prospero must accept at the play's end. Because a damaged sibling is always a disavowed part of self, I believe every intact sibling must come to terms with the Caliban within in order to become fully human. Understanding the influence that such a sibling inevitably has on one's destiny is an essential—and frequently avoided—task.

Whatever their relationship in the external world, damaged siblings loom large in the internal world of their normal brothers and sisters, as manifested in the four symptoms of the Caliban Syndrome that this book examines:

- Premature maturity
- Survivor guilt

- ◆ Compulsion to achieve
- ◆ Fear of contagion

The Caliban Syndrome has an impact far beyond the immediate families of the disabled and the difficult. These relationships are an exaggeration of the dynamics of every sibling relationship, which like every other human bond always has its dark side. Disconnecting internally from unacceptable aspects of a sibling is as universal as the primordial emotions these relationships evoke, and we pay a price for amputating them. Without acknowledging hate and repudiation, we can never truly love ourselves or anyone else; superficial assertions that short-circuit the full intensity of these prohibited emotions never work. Neither does professing spiritual uplift or sugarcoating the lifelong rigors and frustrations of having your closest relative never be your peer. Acknowledged or not, growing up with a difficult or damaged sibling is one of the defining experiences of a person's life.

The disabled and their parents have much-needed advocates; until now their siblings have had practically none. In their behalf, I take issue with the current politically correct euphemism "special needs" children because I believe that all children have special needs. Compassion for the extraordinary trials their families endure and admiration for their achievements should not blind us to the damage done by ignoring the toll on their normal siblings. I use the terms *normal*, *abnormal*, *intact*, and *damaged* not to make value judgments but to reflect more accurately the point of view of higher-functioning siblings, who typically live in an environment that requires them to suppress taboo emotions, judgments, and the evidence of their senses. Idealizing their lives as somehow ennobling, and concomitantly denigrating and denying that there is indeed such a thing as normality (with all its contradictions and complications), damages everybody and leads to dangerous self-estrangement in society as a whole.

No one with an abnormal sibling has a normal childhood. Consciously or unconsciously, every intact sibling is haunted by the fear of catching the disability, a fear that always has a modicum of psychological truth. Family gatherings and significant events become occasions for anxiety and suppressed shame. Cheerful caretakers, mature before their time, they are supposed to consider themselves lucky to be normal. They feel tormented by the compulsion to compensate for their parents' disappointments by having no problems and making no demands, and they are often unaware of the massive external and internal pressure to pretend that nothing is amiss. Their success is always tainted by their sibling's failure, their future clouded by an untoward sense of obligation and responsibility. Their goal is to be as different from their sibling as possible. They live forever in the shadow of the one who does not function.

It is not my intent to create a new category of victim; the Suffering Olympics already has a surfeit of contenders, and I believe passionately that defining yourself as a victim—no matter what you have endured—is the opposite of insight, and actually perpetuates the ordeal by cutting off the possibility of integrating and overcoming it. In fact, one of the most striking characteristics of these siblings is their lack of complaint and their tendency to hide from themselves the burdens that their very normality has placed on them. I want them to know and others to appreciate what they, and those like them, experience.

*   *   *

THE BOOK BEGINS with the story of my relationship with my own older brother, who was emotionally troubled from childhood on and also became seriously ill as an adult. It reflects the guilt, the grief, and the self-knowledge I have gained from my ongoing struggle to overcome my resistance and acknowledge his significance in my life. Sixty other "normal ones" aged seventeen to seventy-five, whose brothers and sisters range from microcephalic to highly obnoxious, tell the poignant, often secret stories of their lives. They also report their powerful and revealing dreams, which have never before been systematically studied for clues about their hidden inner world.

Having a damaged sibling marks you. No matter what you achieve, where you go, or who you love, that other's life remains your secret alternative template, the chasm into which you could plunge if you misstep. Whether you know it or not, his is the doom you dare not duplicate, the fate you contemplate with shame, guilt, secret envy, and—always—relief. You are ashamed that you are related, guilty that you have a better life, envious that nothing is expected of him, relieved that you are not the misfit to be scorned or pitied. Because a sibling is your closest relative, you are eternally enmeshed with each other. Your sanity and stability are forever suspect. You can consciously disconnect your destinies, but you cannot sever the fundamental tie because it embodies the disavowed part of your history and character with which you must come to terms or never truly know yourself. I hope this book eases and illuminates the way.

PART I

Where Have All the Siblings Gone?

chapter 1

My Brother, Myself

the stranger in the attic: steven and me

ALTHOUGH I HAVE AN OLDER BROTHER, I have always been an only child. We grew up in the same house, had the same parents and the same coloring. I spent my entire childhood with him, but I don't remember one shared moment, one heart-to-heart conversation. I never looked up to him, never mentioned him in any of the voluminous diaries I've kept or in either of the books I've written. I own no photograph of him, no keepsake. Having a sibling has been an abstract, oddly detached concept for me rather than a real experience.

How desperately I've worked to keep it that way.

My brother Steven—even now it feels strange to call him

that—was the classic problem child: obese, truculent, picked on by his peers, and troublesome to his teachers. He fought constantly with our parents, who could not conceal that he was an embarrassment and a burden; I was their darling and delight. He flunked out of college; I excelled. He barely made a living; I became Dr. Safer, like our father. His wretched marriage disintegrated; mine was profiled in *Life*. My innate superiority was as just and natural as slavery felt to slave owners. He seemed a changeling, an absence, or an inconvenience—a disruption to my family rather than a member of it. In reality he was a warning: my dark and dreaded opposite.

Only when I visited him in the hospital in 1999 after one of his legs was amputated because of advanced diabetes—he lost the other as well the following year—did I begin to reconsider our relationship or indeed realize that we had one. A man much more than seven years older than I, his eyes full of weariness, sat in a wheelchair, surprisingly glad to see me. The determination and courage in his demeanor, the urgency and undiminished joy with which he spoke of wanting to lead his dance band again (his musical ability was the one talent in which he had always clearly surpassed me), put me to shame. Although subsequent interactions proved far more problematic, and too much damage had been done for anything consistently positive to flourish, I finally knew I had a brother.

This encounter, the first after years of obliviousness broken only by occasional pro forma birthday cards and visits kept as short as decently possible by both of us, provoked what may have been my first dream about him, from which I awoke in terror: he was trying to rape me. I experienced his reappearance in my life as a violent invasion of my inner world from which I could no longer exclude him. It is the only nightmare I have ever welcomed.

*   *   *

IN MY SUBSEQUENT SEARCH for any remnant of our shared history, I collected every shred of evidence of Steven's presence I could retrieve, much of it from drawers in my parents' house that had been unopened for decades. I scanned the snapshots, report cards, letters I had written, home movies, and my own minimal memories. *Recovery* is not the right word for this task; so much never registered to begin with. Seeing the paucity of images, the pitifully few mementos or even thoughts about him that I retain, shocks me now as it never did before. It used to feel so unremarkable to have nothing of him in my life; why would you have mementos of somebody who played so little part, who barely entered your consciousness? I always assumed that the gap in our ages and interests made us inhabit nonintersecting worlds, but that was the flimsiest of justifications. The lack of evidence is damning: I made my closest relative disappear. This grossly unfair, inhumane obliteration, which our parents covertly initiated and abetted, does not even qualify as disowning him—that would imply there had been a relationship, even if it were later repudiated. All my life it seemed the most natural thing in the world. Long before computers, I had a highly effective delete key in my psyche.

STEVEN AND I GREW UP in a middle-class Jewish family in Cincinnati, Ohio. We were both planned and were born seven years apart; World War II intervened. Our (using that inclusive plural pronoun makes us seem more related than I ever felt) father was a shy and diligent anesthesiologist, our mother the consummate suburban "homemaker" with an artistic flair. Our parents, generous children of immigrants, had the intellectual and economic aspirations of their generation and strove to give their own children the best of everything. Consequently, we had the music lessons, the birthday parties, the summer vacations complete with annual pilgrimages to New York City and its boutiques of children's clothes that were the external trappings of successful family life.

There were minefields in this landscape that I discovered only later. My father had several bouts of serious illness—ulcerative colitis around the time of Steven's birth, cardiac symptoms when I was a year old (he was told then that a faulty heart valve would kill him within the year, although he lived thirty-one more), and nearly fatal peritonitis that kept him hospitalized three months when I was ten and Steven was finishing high school. Our parents' marriage, cozy and playful in my early years, fell apart spectacularly in my adolescence—not coincidentally, right after Steven left for college.

In examining the photographs I unearthed, I was struck by how few, other than the class pictures everybody bought, depicted Steven after age two. This is telling because my father was a skilled and prolific amateur photographer; there were plenty of shots of me. In the only portrait of us together, I am less than a year old, and it was obviously posed. He seems to have morphed from an unusually beautiful blond toddler with a winning smile and an exquisite outfit into a downcast, already overweight seven-year-old. The pictures confirm my memory: I never saw him laugh. There was but one happy Polaroid, added to the collection within the last twenty years, of Steven in middle age, decked out in a bow tie and red-striped vest, leading his band and playing his trumpet with gusto, for an audience of strangers.

Judging from the data, my brother was in trouble before I was born, but my arrival exacerbated it spectacularly. There are families where it is an advantage to be born one sex or the other, and female was definitely the right option in mine; my father could not tolerate a rival, my mother needed a mirror, and I filled the bill for both. Qualities that must have seemed defiant or difficult in him seemed fetching, even inspiring, in me.

The name I was given epitomized my role in the family, which virtually guaranteed a rift between us. My mother called me "Gene," on the theory that, since she expected me to become a writer, I should have a mannish pen name at the ready; her daughter was going to be unusual and had to make it in a man's world. My father sensibly suggested I might prefer the feminine form, "Jeanne," and as in most things, his will prevailed. The original name she chose, even with modifications, presaged my destiny. I was enshrined as the replacement son, the shiny new female version of the hopelessly inadequate boy, whom both my parents unconsciously considered damaged goods to be discarded. Here was a second chance, a child who would not—who dared not—disappoint, whose cleverness and determination were no threat but rather the compensatory source of pride and joy and promise. I was dressed for success in a masculine name, and all their dreams were transferred to me.

My mission was assigned to me along with my name, and I chose to accept it. In their eyes Steven was already a lost cause who unconsciously represented their shortcomings as parents. I was to be the anti-Steven and learned early to define myself as his opposite. My becoming a star would make them stars, and my precocity was lovingly nurtured toward that end. The three of us constituted the perfect family unit, even if achieving it took editing out one member.

Steven was a convenient receptacle for all negativity and strife. We had no problems; he was the problem, and there was no solution. Using a child for this purpose, a popular strategy, is undetectable from within a family. My parents could not see that Steven was starving for their love or that he hated himself for disappointing them. To them he was primarily a hardship to be endured. They were acutely aware that he was abnormal, but they could not bear to think that they had anything to do with it; they rendered themselves as helpless and hopeless as he was. Making someone the embodiment of self-inflicted failure precludes any possibility of growth or healing, even as it absolves you of responsibility. The fault had to be his. To think otherwise would have disrupted their carefully constructed, fragile equilibrium, their sense that they were good people and good parents; it would have brought trouble squarely into paradise.

I don't know what, if anything, was really the matter with Steven, other than having the wrong parents. Although he had no intellectual deficit, the school problems apparent in even his earliest report cards—the low grades in conduct, the repeated Steven-could-try-harders—would suggest a learning disability or attention deficit disorder today. He got in no terrible trouble and tended to get beaten up rather than to beat up others, although he did fight physically with his girlfriends later. Depression, obesity, and isolation, never drugs or criminality, plagued him.

At home his misery was manifested in constant turmoil; *sullen* and *surly* best describe his predominant moods. He fought with my parents all the time, about nothing in particular, although his grades, his weight, his "laziness," and his choice of companions were reasons for dispute. At the dinner table, from childhood through adolescence, silence alternated with fits of rage, and spectacular exits were the norm. He seemed at a continual simmer and would strike out for no apparent reason. My mother counterattacked; my father withdrew or pleaded for peace that never came. On one vacation when he was a teenager (I always shared their room and he stayed alone), he became so furious—again I have no idea why—that he insisted on getting a train ticket home. There was relief all around when he left.

One of the ways my parents demonstrated that they had given up on Steven was by making no concerted or effective efforts to discipline him when he sulked or raged. They treated him as though he were a force of nature whose outbursts could only be weathered. This sent him the message that he was exempt from basic rules of conduct, which reinforced his conviction that he was unsocializable. I was expected to back them up by sitting quietly through the storms and the quiet-before-the-storms that ruined every family occasion. They felt unable to control him, so they never taught him to control himself.

Although I hated his outbursts, I secretly envied his freedom to indulge in them. He didn't have to behave, and he suffered no consequences. When you have no position, you have no position to lose.

Nobody set proper limits with Steven until five years ago when, over my mother's silent protest, I said at a dinner that I would leave the restaurant if he maintained his angry silence. It felt like a dangerous breach of etiquette. I was fifty years old.

In hindsight I realize that his obnoxiousness and the tension he created so alienated me that I could not notice, and did not wish to see, his underlying anguish and despair. I could not stand to know that Steven had no other way of calling attention to himself or fending others off. Not knowing how to please, he could only provoke.

Although undoubtedly my brother was chronically enraged at me as well, I remember no untoward violence between us; he would certainly have been blamed and punished for any fights we had, since I was so much younger and more devious. My only scary memory is his having shown me a picture in a storybook that frightened me horribly at age five—it was terrifying enough that I opened the same book with embarrassed trepidation at age thirty-five.

Why did my parents, with their medical sophistication, not intervene? My mother, at least, noticed that something was gravely amiss and begged my father to get psychiatric help for Steven; family therapy would of course have been unthinkable. My father, disdaining the profession, flatly refused; he was probably too ashamed at the prospect of exposure before his colleagues. To this day my mother has not forgiven herself for capitulating.

The most startling exclusionary act my parents ever committed, the one Steven never recovered from, was a decision they made about our living arrangements. For the better part of five years, from the age of eleven, he actually stayed by himself in the attic, separated from my parents and me by another apartment on the intervening floor.

On the surface it was a perfectly rational temporary solution, dictated by necessity. We were living in a cramped two-bedroom apartment on the ground floor of a house owned by my father's parents, who occupied the second floor. My mother frantically tried various arrangements, but a prepubescent boy and his baby sister could share a bedroom for only so long, and nobody could sleep comfortably in the living room, so Steven had to be moved to the third floor. My father concurred for reasons rooted in his past. He refused to move out of his parents' house even after he could easily have afforded his own; we constantly looked at real estate, but no place met his exacting standards. His flamboyantly handsome, far more sociable older brother, also a doctor, had been shamelessly preferred by their mother, and he must have thought he could finally get some attention from that smart, imperious, and cold woman by living downstairs from her. Though my mother agonized over this decision, she felt she had no choice. Her fears of abandonment, and memories of brutal arguments between her own parents, prevented her from taking a stand in Steven's behalf; marital harmony had to be preserved, and he was the casualty.

Both my parents were driven by buried needs that made them disregard the consequences of their plan. Only after four years did my father finally decide to build a house, but by the time it was finished and Steven had his own room, he was ready to leave home for college and for good.

Guilt prompted my mother to furnish Steven's hideaway with everything a boy could desire. His banishment was not at all strange to me—the place seemed glamorous, exotic, and blissfully private (solitude was the one commodity I had too little of), and I don't remember his objecting. But he was an outcast, the stranger in the attic. Every night, cut off from his family, he slept all by himself on the third floor in lonely luxury, while they, safely ensconced with their good child, lived in artificial happiness below.

My brother's exile to the attic simply made evident what had long been the unspoken truth: there was no place for him with us. I never imagined he was miserable up there, though my mother later lamented that he cried when he climbed the stairs at night. His snug den probably also became a retreat from the uninviting family circle two floors down. Still, he must have felt utterly abandoned, the physical barrier fortifying the psychological one that was by then impenetrable. He was to stay on a different level for the rest of his life.

Separating Steven from the family was intended—unconsciously, of course—to remove the source of all ills. Although superficially life did become more tranquil in our charmed circle when he wasn't around, exorcising him had ominous implications for me that I have never escaped. With a child's logic I figured out that he was ostracized because he was bad; this made the consequences of being anything like him dangerously real. What if I lost my temper once too often, got a less than stellar grade, gained too much weight—failed at anything? What if I relaxed my guard and my charm or my competence crashed? Could the same thing happen to me if I no longer measured up? Just to be on the safe side, I made many mental additions to the list of things I dared not be: unhappy, whiny, demanding—anything that could be thought of as childish. One false step, and I could lose everything too. I understood none of this at the time.

Failing was an all-too-real threat because my emotional life was far from ideal, even though (and also because) I was the chosen one. I never consciously connected my imperfections with Steven, but I was terribly aware of them; it must have been easier for me to feel normal because he was so visibly abnormal. I was physically awkward and prone to what I now identify as anxiety and depression, although, luckily, I loved school. And so acclimated was I to the company of adults that I never felt entirely comfortable with other children. While I was never scorned, I was never popular either; I have felt like an outsider all my life. What saved me is that I knew how to make my parents happy.

How could these people, both of whom were decent and capable of devotion, have treated their son so badly? They tried to support him later and would not have dreamed of literally disinheriting him. At critical moments they came to his aid; my mother persuaded the dean of his college to readmit Steven, and he graduated. But because they blamed him for their own inability to relate to him, the damage they did was profound. The traumas of their childhoods, the troubled relationships with their own parents and siblings, of which they were unaware, drove them to it. Their behavior, rather than malevolent, was tragically blind and misguided.

My father, such an adoring presence when I was a little girl, withdrew from Steven early on. Only once do I remember the two of them attending an activity alone together—a baseball game that neither especially enjoyed. My mother was the more engaged parent, who fought some battles for him and took care of him when he was ill, but she could never listen to him. She alternated between blaming him and blaming herself.

Steven had the misfortune to be a bad reflection, in both senses of the term, on each of his parents. In him they saw sides of themselves they shrank from rather than what all parents yearn to see—an image of their better selves. It was a terrible fit.

His mother had to have a child who emulated her, whose talents and temperament matched hers, and whose successes fulfilled her frustrated aspirations. To justify her life, she needed somebody in whose glory she could shine. Steven showed her she was a failure.

For his father, Steven represented qualities that he detested in himself and that his own mother had repudiated—shyness, depression, and emotional hunger. Though he had been slender as a young man, he had gained some weight himself by the time he had a family. He could find in his son none of the academic brilliance, discipline, and self-containment on which he prided himself and for which he was valued. He had always lived in the shadow of his own brother, and he put Steven there too. And having lost his mother's love to a rival, he would not tolerate another; he and he alone would be the masculine center of attention for his wife. He was reproducing the pattern in his own family, only this time he did the rejecting. Steven was too much like his father's own nightmare vision of himself, the awful truth that even professional success could not undo. His son was a more fitting receptacle for his self-hatred than his daughter. Steven shamed him.

That both my parents were youngest children, with older brothers, also made it easier for them to identify with me.

I had my own reasons for being their willing accomplice, and an agent in my own right, in the secret campaign to keep the Safer family Steven-free. I helped erase him to ensure that I would remain the focus of attention. Instinctively, since his life was a cautionary tale of the consequences of failing to please, I kept myself up by putting him down, calling attention to his deficits and my own assets. I had to denigrate Steven to reinforce my superiority, which otherwise would have been in doubt.

I am struck by how utterly lacking in empathy or compassion for him I was, and how I never felt the slightest twinge of guilt for being so blatantly favored over my brother. Why didn't I try to relate to him? Family dynamics kept us apart. I needed to see our parents in the same flattering light they shined on themselves, and appreciating Steven's perspective would have ruptured our bond. Any relationship between us would have upset the family and my place therein and highlighted qualities of my own that threatened to destroy everything I had.

One of my very few early-childhood memories related to Steven has always disturbed me because it exposes an unsavory effort to maintain my status at his expense: when I was probably five years old and Steven was sick, I used his toothbrush once, hoping to catch his cold and usurp the unusual amount of attention that was being lavished on him because he was sick. There was something desperate as well as calculating in the gesture; perhaps my exalted position was not as unassailable as I thought. I did not want him taking up residence among us again, even temporarily, so unbeknownst to anyone, I took an extra precaution to make sure he stayed in his place. In a family that practices exclusion, even a station as secure as mine never feels entirely solid, because it rests on the unstable foundation of parents' favor as well as on the miseries of another.

My collusion with my parents and my efforts to reinforce my superiority continued after we had both left home. In a letter I wrote them from college, I commiserated with my mother about the most recent havoc Steven was wreaking, in the coldly self-righteous language I had so thoroughly imbibed over the years that it had become formulaic:

> What can be done with a person like this? How do you instill self-reliance and strength of character, or even raw endurance, in someone so buried in bitterness and failure on every possible level?

In many ways my strategy paid off handsomely. I brought out the best in my parents, particularly before I sought my independence as an adolescent and broke the magic circle. The cost became apparent only recently: it robbed me of my brother and of part of myself.

Despite the serious failings of his family, Steven himself is ultimately responsible for his fate; even as a child he was no martyred innocent. He overcame some of his liabilities after he left home, but he remained mired in bitterness, recriminations, and entitled victimhood. These attitudes are never confined to one's family alone. He also neglected himself physically and for years avoided any sort of therapy; in both habits he was, unfortunately, his father's son. My parents and I contributed mightily to his sorrows, but his own choices perpetuated them.

The one thing they did right was foster Steven's musical talent. Appreciation of music and the ability to make it was one thing the four of us genuinely had in common, even if we never enjoyed it together. They let him experiment with instruments—even a drum set—until he discovered the trumpet, and then patiently went through candidates until they found the right teacher for him—a man whose name and benign influence I still remember. He was the only one of us ever to play professionally. We attended his performances, where I had the unfamiliar experience of seeing Steven in the spotlight. He was featured in his high school show, wearing a pith helmet and playing "Tiger Rag"; I would later audition to sing in mine but never made the cut. Music has been his rampart through every hardship. This is something we share, but he does not know we do.

Unfortunately for both of them, my father, who played a mellow clarinet and saxophone, never played duets with his son, though he clearly inspired him. Steven still performs the music my father loved, big band hits of World War II vintage, along with jazz of many eras. It is the sole unambivalently positive bond they had.

Steven's pivotal position in our family became clear only when he left, and all the pathology he had contained over the years spilled out. It is no accident that our parents' marriage then imploded and my relationship with my mother exploded; the effort of keeping him at bay had united us. So well did we hide his role in plain sight that I only noticed it recently; it had worked like a charm.

During the wretched tumult of my parents' separation, I turned to Steven for help for the only time in my life, but by then it was too late. I called him at college and he rebuffed me, saying my mother was paranoid and my father above reproach.

ALTHOUGH STEVEN FOUND SATISFACTIONS and compensations in subsequent years, trials both mental and physical were added to his childhood tribulations. His marriage failed, he had limited success as an insurance agent, and diabetes struck in his thirties, a baleful paternal legacy. Steven endured bypass surgery at age forty, was too ill to work by age fifty, and by age sixty had lost all kidney function and both his legs. He ended up spending more time in the hospital than out of it. Because of our estrangement, he never turned to me for comfort.

Though beset with problems, Steven had a better time in life outside the family than he ever had within it. He longed for family connections and found them among our father's relatives. He made friends who stood by him and finally met a woman who was devoted to him and who saw him through his devastating illnesses.

He led his dance band, by now a weekly fixture in the city, through everything and started to sing in it as well. He hosted a radio show featuring the music he loved.

Far more gregarious and civic-minded than anyone else in the family, he joined community groups and rose to the top in several of them. Fraternal organizations became the center of his life; he was president of the brotherhood of his temple and a prominent member of Big Brothers, the men's organization that helps fatherless boys. He found symbolic ways to be a brother, having never been mine.

But he recently got a sickening and gratuitous reminder that his earlier exclusion from his family would never end. Two years ago our mother, at age eighty-seven, moved to a nursing home in the early stage of Alzheimer's disease. (Our father had died years before.) When Steven went for the first time to visit her there, the staff refused to admit him. According to their records, her only child was a daughter. She had not told them she had a son.

the dark mirror: steven in me

When I was a child, I spake as a child, I understood as a child, I thought as a child: but when I became a man, I put away childish things.

For now we see through a glass, darkly; but then face to face: now I know in part but then shall I know even as also I am known.

I Corinthians

As I began to reconsider my brother and myself, all I felt—when I felt anything at all—was shame and shrinking away from him and from qualities in myself that evoked him. Fear lurked behind the shame. I was conscious of not wanting to be like him, but I had no idea how deep my repudiation went, how much it shaped my life, and how impossible a task it really was. As I understood more, the shame (at least the part about how I regarded him) turned to guilt, tempered with frustration. As my empathy for Steven grew, I felt more compassion for the ways I resemble him. Now much has melted into sorrow and a sense of irredeemable loss.

I had a long way to go. Only three years before, when I was in my brother's hospital room and the nurse addressed him as "Mr. Safer," a preposterous thought went through my head: who is this man? Of course I would have recognized "Mrs. Safer" (my mother) and "Dr. Safer" (my father, my uncle, or myself), but here was a startling and unfamiliar prefix to the family surname. So little time had I spent in Steven's company as an adult, so little did I know him or see him with other people, that I had never heard his name before. My reaction mimicked the scene in *The Bald Soprano,* Ionesco's absurdist play, in which two people upon meeting keep remarking "How bizarre! And what a strange coincidence!" as the accumulating details they trade about their lives lead inexorably to the conclusion that they are husband and wife. In the original production, my edition notes, "this dialogue was spoken and played in a style sincerely tragic," as it deserves.

*   *   *

I AWOKE THE DAY I started to write about Steven from a startling dream:

> I keep trying to sharpen my pencil, but I can't get the sharpener to work. I'm struggling to regain consciousness, fighting through a haze that seems almost viscous, as though I'm drugged and waking up from anesthesia. Then I hear water running ominously and rush into my office. There is evidence of a major leak in the corner, but I don't know where it's coming from. I try frantically to get someone to fix it.

This dream, which seemed compellingly real, revealed how conflicted I felt about telling our story. As much as I needed to record it, I was frightened of how I would feel; writing makes things inescapably real. I was fighting to wake up to the truth, but it was still a battle not to remain unconscious about our connection; there had to be good reasons why I had always concealed it from myself. The dream told me that the defenses I used to prevent Steven from "leaking" into my life were not impermeable. The carefully constructed identity that I had hermetically sealed off from his dangerous influence—epitomized by the room where I work as a professional psychoanalyst—was no longer secure.

I never doubted that my nonrelationship with my brother was peculiar and that it set me apart from what most other siblings feel for one another; this was just a piece of information noted in passing, nothing consciously envied or longed for. His absence in my life hardly registered; in order to miss something, you have to see its value, and it was critical for me to devalue him. For most people with brothers and sisters, being a sibling is as implicit a part of their identity as stature—not something they think about every day but a basic fact. It was never part of mine. Being Steven's sibling got relegated to the attic of my consciousness. This didn't seem odd to me, although people are always surprised to learn of his existence. I became proficient at discounting him so early that I never noticed the effort.

Thinking about our connection, or being reminded of it, has made me uncomfortable for as long as I can remember. Once when I told a therapist that I strove to be Steven's opposite and was asked to enumerate the traits I fled, I felt almost physical resistance to identifying them, as though "fat, angry, unpopular, unsuccessful" might stick to me if I said the words aloud. In my long years of psychotherapy, many issues subliminally related to him got resolved, though Steven barely surfaced again directly. Still, I was immensely relieved that he could not attend my wedding, which spared me from having to introduce him to people. Although I told myself differently, I shunned Steven because his being, not his behavior, embarrassed me; he gave the lie to my mental health.

My urgency to differentiate myself from him in mind and body (though the family resemblance has actually gotten stronger as we have aged) was based on a very real threat: every day, on the third floor, I observed the consequences of failing to fulfill the mandate. To be physically unappealing, emotionally immature, or burdensome would shame me in my parents' eyes and might exile me too forever from their favor. Efforts to excel on all fronts, begun on their behalf, continued on my own.

Not only do I drive myself to perform; I have to make it look easy. As Steven's counterweight, I embodied success as he embodied the reverse; it was what I was, not something I should, or could, work at. So proficient have I become that a patient of mine lamented that even the flowers in my vase arranged themselves effortlessly. The unglamorous source of this art is my assumption that people will abandon me if I fail to live up to their expectations.

What worried me most was always threatening to come true. Anxiety that I would turn into Steven has pursued me from childhood on, though never identified as such. I tried to shape my personality to be immune to his flaws. These exertions have been so pervasive and so underground that I can only track them by seeing how unsettled I am when they falter and I see him in my mirror.

Assaults on my body image are the worst, because Steven's body was considered so out of control, the visible reason he was rejected at home and at school. My own too-ample belly, which in middle age seems to have expanded inordinately and resists all efforts to make it contract, fills me with disproportionate humiliation and despair. Though I never developed an eating disorder, I feel as little sympathy toward myself for being moderately overweight as my parents conveyed to Steven. Every woman in America agonizes over the size of her thighs, but few have concrete cause to think that excess flesh could cause them to be exiled from their own families. In mine Steven's weight was not a symptom or even an affliction; it was the stigma of a flawed nature.

Internal dangers alarm me as much as overt ones. For a person whose health has been blessedly robust and who works to keep it so—another way not to emulate my brother—I am always afraid that I too could be prone to life-threatening illnesses or that mild ones will turn dire. Heredity is destiny, I warn myself, and I generalize its potential for harm. When anything goes wrong with my body, my moods, my work, or my social life, I search for signs of disaster. Everything seems tenuous; my footing is forever perilous. Anxiety does not rule me or paralyze me, and it has been tempered by years of therapy, but panic is still my reflexive response to uncertainty.

I now recognize that these troubling fantasies are manifestations of the guilt I escaped in childhood, my punishment for having a better life. Unconsciously I believe that my achievements intentionally caused my brother to fail. Now the one who used to feel entitled to everything does not think she deserves even the successes she has worked diligently to achieve. I prevent myself from enjoying victory too much by thinking that defeat is just around the corner.

Pessimism is the harshest, most persistent legacy of being Steven's sister. If something is even a little wrong, I assume it's rotten to the core; like a cold, a temporary setback could signal the beginning of a relentless downward spiral. This attitude doesn't interfere with my efforts, but it mars my pleasure and satisfaction and makes relaxation elusive. Curiously I reserve negativity exclusively for myself; for everybody else I am an enthusiastic proponent of the power to change through insight, work, and will. A paradoxical combination of exuberance, resilience, and catastrophic expectation coexist in my temperament.

Because I am so demanding of myself and regard my own emotional and physical imperfections with the same abhorrence that Steven evoked, I do not assume I can count on compassion from others, and I am always relieved and grateful to be proved wrong. It is hard not to expect that if I seem depressed or unproductive those I love or admire will give up on me, just as I feared my parents would turn away if I veered too close to Steven.

In my darkest moments I used to feel a nameless dread. The content of that dread is clear to me now: the image of Steven that my family created is the awful truth about me, the Caliban within, whom I fight to conceal from everyone.

STEVEN, WHO SO RECENTLY SEEMED to have nothing to do with my destiny, in fact has played an unacknowledged role in every significant choice I have made. Arranging my life to circumvent or repair the problems he caused, or to prevent a repetition, has been my unconscious agenda.

Steven is one of the reasons I chose to be childless, although other factors influenced this decision, and avoidance was not my principal motivation. My fear of having a child like him was a projection of my fear of becoming him myself, deflected onto the next generation. I was also afraid of becoming Steven's mother, mired in guilt and self-recrimination because her son felt so alien, and feeling incapable of nurturing him. I got the best of what my parents had to offer, but family life as I knew it was not an experience I was in a hurry to reproduce.

Steven was not irrelevant to my becoming a psychoanalyst, my chosen vocation since childhood. Making a difference to others as I never could to him was a form of surrogate reparation, as well as a way to transform the amorphous anxiety we lived in by understanding it. The optimistic side of my nature needed to disprove my parents' unspoken dictum that his problems could never be solved. And earning a doctorate made me even more my father's heir. No wonder that whenever I suggested to Steven that he go into therapy, he was insulted and considered my heartfelt plea condescending.

How my brother behaved affected what I sought and fled in relationships. Because of him I became unduly sensitive to the silent treatment, or even slightly raised voices, and completely intolerant of tantrums. It is essential for me to feel understood because Steven never was. I have also always sought substitute brothers and treasure the love of my male friends as the compensation for the bond I forfeited with him.

My image of my brother has never been entirely watertight. There are fragments of evidence about him that do not fit my family's gloomy perception, but I used to patch the "leaks" quickly; when the designated receptacle of negativity does something positive, the world turns upside down. He has devoted himself to causes and gets along fine with people outside his immediate family; how can the problem have been all his?

So intent have I been on making myself different from Steven that I neglected to notice the positive things we have in common; it is impossible to see someone clearly if you are always busy running in the opposite direction. I share my brother's love of music and delight in performing it. And the determination—some might even say stubbornness—on which I pride myself pales beside his valiant battle to express himself musically and give joy to others despite the physical suffering he endures every day. It is an exceptional feat of bravery that I can only hope to emulate.

I still feel shame when I think about Steven, but the focus has changed. I am no longer embarrassed to be related to him; I am ashamed of how I regarded him. The guilt I never felt has also become unavoidable. He was the family scapegoat, and I colluded to keep him so. I cannot reverse the favoritism that was undeserved, nor the ways it distorted both our lives and prevented any trust or real love from developing between us. I do not pity him as an inferior; I grieve because my closest relative was and always will be far too distant from me.

It feels impossible to be myself with Steven. I once thought about calling him to let him know I was going to be on television, but I had no idea how he would respond. Would he feel like I was rubbing his nose in my success if I told him, or be offended if I did not? No spontaneous gesture seems possible, only second-guessing and management. I, who pride myself on sensitivity and understanding, draw a blank when it comes to him.

Several months ago a bout of illness forced me to cancel a longed-for vacation. For the first time it dawned on me that my brother has never had a real one since the unhappy trips he took with our family forty years ago, while I have been all over the world. Such sickening contrasts in our fortunes, once a source of secret relief, now only pain me.

When I went back to Cincinnati two years ago to close up the house our parents had finally built, the one in which Steven briefly had a proper room of his own, I saw once more how conspicuous he was by his absence. He wanted none of their possessions, only a few trinkets he had bought on a trip we took in the early 1960s; there was nothing that bore any relation to him or that he felt attached to. He never had a real home as long as I can remember, and he now lives by himself in a cluttered apartment still furnished with the dresser and night tables that had been his consolation prize in the attic. I wept because he had so few happy moments or memories there and none of them with me.

The day I visited him in the hospital after his leg was amputated changed forever the way I experienced my brother. I saw strength of character, a passion for living, and a capacity for endurance in him that made me feel proud, and I told him so. These qualities had to have been latent in him all the time of our childhood, unappreciated by his family.

Soon afterward we had the first real conversation of our lives. He said, through tears, that he did not want us to be unreconciled, and I welcomed the opportunity with tears of my own. I told him that I had been unfairly favored and that it had not been good for me either, which seemed to surprise him. I said I was glad he had found more love in adulthood than he had gotten in childhood, that though we couldn't change history, we could still have something real together, and he seemed to want to try.

But it did not last. He retreated back into the familiar sullen shell and repulsed any efforts to coax him out; he would not, or could not, muster the energy to engage with me and let me into his life at this late date. Perhaps he did not trust my sincerity or want to open up the past again. Maybe he prefers anger to anguish and finds it easier to be alienated than grief-stricken about what we never had.

After the terrorist attack in New York on September 11, he called to make sure I was unharmed, but he didn't want to talk to me.

There will be no "closure" in this relationship, at least not between us. The only transformation I can count on has already occurred, within me. The reconciliation he said he desired may be out of reach, and I may never be much more than the chip on my brother's shoulder.

Even if we never meet again, Steven is indelible to me now. In my mind at least we both have three dimensions now and, since I finally have the capacity, the possibility of some remnant of a real relationship. And though I know the odds are against it, I hope we can have even a little time as brother and sister before we lose each other forever so soon after finding each other for the first time. We would get something precious that has been missing in our lives. The irony is almost unbearable; I hate to see that just as I acknowledge how much he is a part of me, he refuses to acknowledge me as part of him. Just when I can give something genuine of myself, he insists I still offer nothing. As soon as I discover him, he makes himself disappear, this time by his own choice.

Now that I see through the glass less darkly, I long to be face to face with him, to be known even as I know. But that is not to be. He hides from me. Turning the tables is the only power he thinks he can wield over me; to be thought inhumane when I appreciate his humanity at last is my punishment. Who can blame him? It was true for too long. I accept his rejection, though it grieves me. I will carry it to my grave. I am glad I finally know the truth. The leaks in my office will never be repaired again; I don't want them fixed. This is the achievement I'm proud of, and my consolation.

chapter 2

Everybody's an
Only Child

FACING HOW I BURIED MY BROTHER'S ROLE in my life has been an ordeal; I now understand why I avoided it for fifty-four years. To broaden my perspective—both out of professional interest and because studying emotional experience has always been the way I cope with it—I surveyed psychological studies of siblings. Extensive research turned up practically nothing, even in the psychoanalytic literature, my own specialty, which focuses specifically on what is hidden and expelled from awareness. To my astonishment, I discovered that the resistance and disconnection I battled in myself also pervades my profession; psychoanalysis, the talking cure, is strangely silent about siblings.

"Siblings" does not appear in the 404-page index to the twenty-three-volume *Standard Edition* of Freud—there are a mere five citations for "brothers and sisters"—but "Siberia" does. The founder of psychoanalysis symbolically relegated his own seven siblings there and set the precedent for his followers to ignore the influence of their own and their patients' closest kin to this day. The major textbooks in the field followed suit, focusing virtually exclusively on relations between parents and children. No panel on siblings had yet been held at a scientific meeting and only a handful of articles were published in psychoanalytic journals as late as 1980, three generations after Freud first wrote about the power of the unconscious and the centrality of early family experience. Eloise Agger called attention to this omission in her 1983 paper "Psychoanalytic Perspectives on Sibling Relationships," and now another quarter-century has passed with nary a comprehensive study in print; without accumulated data, the occasional articles that do appear reinvent the wheel. Scientific literature outside the psychoanalytic tradition is similarly scant, although siblings are more conspicuous in imaginative literature and biography, where the taboo seems to have less power.

How and why have siblings escaped scrutiny? Everybody, clinicians and theorists included, wants to be an only child. This desire was compelling for Freud and had subtle but major impact on his theoretical formulations. An adored firstborn son, he never got over his guilty triumph that his unwelcome nine-month-old younger brother died when Freud was one and a half years old; later he noted that this experience had left him with "the germ of self-reproach" and had "determined what is neurotic, and also what is intense, in all my friendships." His mother had six more children, all daughters, before his tenth birthday. Hostility among siblings, he wrote, is "far more frequent in childhood than the unseeing eye of adult observers can perceive." Yet it is imperceptible in the Oedipus complex, in which a son's only rival for his mother's love is his father. All younger potential competitors (particularly dead ones of the same sex) are peremptorily disposed of. Despite his own favored position—his eldest sister's piano was given away because the noise of her playing bothered him—Freud unwittingly recapitulated sibling rivalry all his life. His tumultuous relationships with friends and colleagues were marred by his need to be the center of attention, his jealousy of potential usurpers, and his sensitivity to betrayal.

Freud's blind spot has been incorporated into the discipline he founded, and his followers, mostly siblings themselves, have been eliminating rivals ever since. As much as it has changed since the early days, psychoanalytic theory still emphasizes parent/child interactions, which leads to training and clinical practice that emphasize parent/child interactions. This vicious cycle keeps every new generation of clinicians blind and deaf to what was originally excluded; even now siblings rarely merit more than informal discussion in case presentations, and it is an unusual analysis in which they receive enough attention. Sibling conflicts of their own prevent most therapists from recognizing the omission and make them collude with their patients to avoid addressing them in depth. They consider it normal, and fail to inquire, if patients never mention a sibling by name or at all or act as though the person were an extra rather than a costar in the drama of their lives. My own treatment is typical; in fifteen years of intensive work, I spent no more than fifteen minutes discussing my brother, and my analyst, whom I later learned had a borderline sister herself, never noticed. Her own efforts to differentiate herself from this sister must have made her consider my attitude as a natural, reasonable fact of life rather than an anxiously constructed and precariously maintained compulsion. The process is insidious and almost undetectable: you find what you look for and ignore what you do not want to see, and you can only help others know what you can recognize in yourself. In professions as in families, avoidance begets avoidance. This is why the psychology of siblings remains terra incognita.

If feelings about even normal siblings are buried, feelings about abnormal ones are buried much more deeply. Therefore I believe that the disproportionate number of people with damaged siblings who become psychotherapists exacerbates the problem. An informal survey of my acquaintances in the field revealed a plethora of hitherto unmentioned dysfunctional sisters and brothers; my colleagues and I are motivated as much by the unconscious need to demonstrate how sane, intact, and different from our siblings we are as by the more conscious vocation to help others.

Personal resistance is not the only factor preventing siblings from getting proper attention. The asymmetrical nature and hierarchical structure of the classical psychoanalytic situation itself (as well as most of its therapeutic siblings), in which the analyst is the authority figure and strives to be a blank screen onto which the patient unilaterally projects internal conflicts, naturally tends to elicit more feelings about parents. As this model shifts to a more egalitarian exchange to which both participants contribute—a development gathering force in the field—siblings may return from their long Siberian sojourn.*

----

*There is some evidence of change. Vamik Volkan and Gabriele Ast, *Siblings in the Unconscious and Psychopathology* (Madison, CT: International Universities Press, 1997) is a recent contribution to the psychoanalytic literature. Salman Akhtar and Selma Kramer, editors, *Brothers and Sisters: Developmental, Dynamic, and Technical Aspects of the Sibling Relationship* (Northvale, New Jersey: Jason Aronson, 1999) is a volume of ground-breaking papers from one of the first psychoanalytic panels on siblings, held at the Twenty-ninth Annual Margaret S. Mahler Symposium on Child Development in 1998.

Now that my own experience has sensitized me to hidden sibling themes, I am struck by how frequently and unexpectedly they appear and how powerfully they affect my patients' relationships with others and with me. Jeremy Mitchell, a young English professor in therapy with me, could not forgive himself for leaving his girlfriend of five years. Though their separation was well considered and civil, he was convinced that he had ruined her prospects and destroyed her self-esteem forever. Visions of her anguished face haunted his dreams. Although she was in fact successful, charming, and independently wealthy, he imagined her living in a trailer park, destitute and alone. He felt he had forfeited his right to visit their familiar haunts, and he avoided streets where she might see him with the new woman in his life. He even contemplated ending his new relationship and returning to the old one to assuage his unbearable guilt and his tormented conviction that he did not deserve to have his own life if it came at another's expense. For months we struggled to understand the inordinate intensity of these feelings, but they did not abate. Only when I began writing this book did I suddenly realize that his crushing sense of responsibility for his girlfriend exactly mirrored his experience with his older sister, who had been anorectic, seriously depressed, and isolated throughout his childhood. His mother had constantly admonished him to keep his sister company and interpreted his natural desire to have an independent life as selfish and destructive—feelings he had internalized and applied to the other woman he felt he had abandoned.

For no apparent reason my patient Mark Monroe impulsively married and instantly conceived a child. My newly developed sibling antennae allowed me to recognize and point out that these events immediately followed the engagement of his preferred, academically successful, but socially inept younger brother whom he had once referred to as "a tough act to precede."

I also became aware that patients can feel like damaged siblings with me. On New Year's Eve Kathy Emerson, an unmarried lawyer about my age, told me how miserable she felt that once again she had no date and would be celebrating with her younger sister and her husband. She always dreaded weekends, staying home because she felt she had no right even to walk on the street alone in a world full of couples. Since she knew I was married, it occurred to me that she must feel envious of me as well. Her distress and implicit envy made me feel terribly uncomfortable, because I knew it was justified; surely she had noticed that in many ways my life was better than hers had ever been. I was luckier than she was; was it not presumptuous and hurtful of me to point this out? My hesitation, I realized, came from guilt masquerading as tact; I sidestepped the topic not because I wanted to spare her but because I wanted to spare myself from her justified wrath; here was another unseemly and undeserved triumph that I dared not enjoy or reveal—much like my earlier, seemingly effortless triumph over my own brother. Then I heard myself asking her a question that seemed almost sacrilegious and that I had never dared to put so baldly before: "How does it feel to know that I have more than you do?" She was profoundly relieved to be granted permission to admit her envy and to describe how shameful, self-hating, and unlovable it made her feel, how it corroded her relationship with her actual sister and with other women. This exchange allowed her to claim more for herself—including, ultimately, a husband of her own.

If, as Joyce's Stephen Daedalus said, "a brother is as easy to lose as an umbrella," why isn't a parent? Try as we might to eliminate them, parents are engraved on our psyches in a way that makes negating their importance far more difficult. They loom so large because they are the first and most prominent figures in every child's life, and we need them to survive. For this reason no therapist would fail to notice if a patient never mentioned a parent or would accept the explanation that a mother's or father's influence was insignificant. Siblings become essential only in extreme situations like death, divorce, or natural disaster when parents are unavailable, and then they are unlikely to be ignored.

When I began research on this book, I discovered that problem siblings are no more popular to talk about than to write about or think about; even the most forthcoming, self-aware people become disturbed, dense, and defensive. I had no trouble finding interview subjects for my two previous books, on choosing not to have children and on resolving intimate betrayal, both topics that can make people anxious and uncomfortable. This time, though, half the people I approached refused, and their explanations made no sense. "It was so long ago that I hardly think of him now. We were five years apart, so I was much more affected by my sister, because she was only a year older," said a woman who had moved three thousand miles away from her autistic brother and left his care to this sister. A man who had frankly described the devastating aftermath of his mother's suicide to me previously pronounced his relationship with his manic-depressive sister "too painful to talk about." Of those who agreed to be interviewed, there was also a dismaying 50 percent dropout rate. A California teacher had eagerly agreed to discuss her troubled, chronically unemployed brother as long as I promised not to identify her family. She sought this reassurance although I had indicated in advance that names and details would be changed. After failing to answer the phone for our interview appointment on three separate occasions, she wrote me a note:

> I realize it was presumptuous of me to be willing to label my brother "dysfunctional." His journey has simply been rich in "dreams deferred." I don't want to demean him or assume that I have prevailed and he hasn't. The last thing I want to do is cause more harm.

Labeling her brother dysfunctional is not presumptuous but objectively accurate, and asserting that she prevailed where he failed is not an assumption but a fact. How will telling the truth that both of them know all too well without naming him cause more harm to her brother? Guilt—for doing better and being glad she did—compels her to euphemize and to protest her good intentions.

"I can't talk about him because he's not here to defend himself," explained a singer whose schizophrenic brother had been missing and presumed dead since 1985. Although she had previously appeared on television to say that fear of passing on her brother's mental illness had made her decide not to have children, to discuss the details of their relationship as siblings even anonymously felt to her like a wantonly aggressive act. It was acceptable to acknowledge their shared genes but not their shared life. She too had a fantasy that to express what she actually thought of him would destroy her brother all over again.

Why are so many people convinced that to tell the story of their siblings is to betray or damage them further? Some are over-identified; sharing a paranoid view of the world is one way to main-

tain some connection and to avoid grasping the strangeness, sadness, and severity of a brother's or sister's pathology. Since it would
be exceedingly unlikely for any sibling to recognize the disguised
source in a book, the normal ones' worries also conceal their wishes;
they fear that even changing names would fail to protect the guilty.

Although a small number of people welcomed an opportunity
to discuss their families and felt gratified that someone was finally
paying attention to them after years of invisibility, distress was a
much more common reaction. Many of the brave souls who
showed up confessed that the prospect of the interview had caused
sleepless nights and anxiety attacks. More than one said that only
their sense of responsibility, desire to be helpful, or devotion to me
prevented them from canceling; their early experiences as dutiful,
mature helpers made them face their fears. A fifty-year-old journal-
ist who had spent years in therapy but had not spoken to his embittered, underachieving sister for a decade explained, "I've attained a
kind of resolution and insulated myself from my family. I finally
have a text for my life, but the spaces between the words are wider
than they ought to be, and that's where she is. If I went in there, the
text is going to get disorganized, and I would have to look at what I
never let myself notice. It would involve a radical revision of my
sense of self. She's the door that never gets opened. I don't dread
very much, but I dreaded thinking about this." Metaphors involving
perilous portals were common; a systems analyst said, "I'm afraid if
I crack open that door, I'll never be able to shut it." No wonder it
stays double-bolted for most of us.

A writer who had chronicled extensively her paranoid sister's
devastating impact on her life and had even performed a one-
woman show in which she spoke in her sister's voice ("It's so much

in my head that it's easy to do," she told me) confessed that the prospect of being interviewed about their relationship was more than she could handle, although why perplexed her. She realized that she was too frightened about what might come out of her mouth and how it might make her feel, when she could not control the content in advance.

Even when reticence is conquered, insight is surprisingly hard to come by. Many people simply recite catalogs of outrageous conduct by siblings that parents had failed to control, behavior they felt subjected to but that seemed to have nothing to do with them. Trouble with their siblings was an external event, something to endure or to flee, that had little effect on their internal reality or sense of themselves. Asked whether he had anything in common with his psychopathic sister, a seventy-year-old executive said, "Absolutely nothing—it's a black and white situation." Sometimes the connections hid in plain sight; an otherwise refreshingly frank and forthcoming therapist whom I interviewed about her paranoid schizophrenic brother noted that her first husband turned out to be paranoid "just like my father." Until I pointed out the similarity, she had never connected him with the brother whose suspiciousness and hostility permeated her life; to do so would have been too close for comfort.

When a relationship deteriorates, even positive memories can be obliterated. A teacher told me that as a young girl she had admired her older half-sister who later behaved hatefully and had a disastrous marriage. Her sister's collection of cashmere sweaters was an image of success, and she used to fantasize that one day she too would own a beautiful blue sweater. She had no idea that she was wearing just such a sweater to our meeting.

*   *   *

NO AMOUNT OF PSYCHIC MANEUVERING can alter the fact that having siblings is one of the defining experiences of childhood, with lifelong reverberations. Children become aware of one another before they recognize their own fathers, and they spend as much time together as they do with either parent. Siblings are your first peers, the first mirror that reflects an image your own size. Their impact does not cease when you leave home. As any adult who attends a family function can attest, the old hierarchy with its familiar but inextricable rules has a dismaying way of reasserting itself. No future tie is exempt from their influence; relations with them are the prototype for friendships, romances, and professional connections with coworkers, rivals, and collaborators for the rest of your life. Ultimately they are the only surviving witnesses to your intimate history. Nobody else will remember your childhood.

PART II

The Burden of Normality

chapter 3

Prospero's Damaged Family

FREUD MAY HAVE MISSED sibling dynamics because of problems of his own, but Shakespeare, whom he esteemed as a precursor, did not. While siblings figure prominently in works from *A Comedy of Errors* to *King Lear*, he portrays relationships in a damaged family with unparalleled insight in *The Tempest*—a theme that, not surprisingly, is rarely noticed; art reveals what science conceals. The relationship between Caliban and Miranda, symbolic siblings in *The Tempest*, resonates deeply for me as an uncannily accurate poetic depiction of my relationship with my own brother. This connection led me to name the syndrome that afflicts all normal ones after Caliban, the archetypal damaged sibling.

Since the magician Prospero, the central figure in *The Tempest* and its author's spokesman, calls the play a dream ("We are such stuff as dreams are made on"), psychoanalytic dream interpretation can illuminate the sibling symbolism in Shakespeare's last work as well as the psychological condition whose name it inspired.

Boundaries of person, time, and space are fluid in the language of dreams, and symbols have multiple meanings. Nothing—words, gestures, sequences of events—is arbitrary. Actions following one another chronologically can signify cause and effect. Everything and everybody in a dream also represent aspects of the self; therefore the play simultaneously depicts the outside world and the protagonist's inner state. Similarly "Caliban" in the Caliban Syndrome is both the abnormal sibling in the normal one's life and an image in the normal one's psyche.

Shakespeare's portraits of Prospero, Caliban, and Miranda plumb the secret depths in one particular type of damaged family—the one I grew up in—and also illustrate themes common to them all. As in our psyches, the relationships among these characters are shifting and multifaceted and are not confined to their literal roles; thus a son (or daughter) is simultaneously a brother, a father, and an aspect of oneself.

The tempest of the title is a magical storm that Prospero, exiled duke of Milan, conjures to bring his treacherous brother Antonio and his entourage to the island where he was shipwrecked, so that moral order can be restored. He lives there with his flawless daughter Miranda, his servant/sprite Ariel, and his "savage and deformed slave" Caliban, who plots to murder him. Prospero creates scenarios to punish and pardon his brother, foil the plot, marry off his daughter, and recover his dukedom. Then, renouncing supernatural powers, he drowns his magic book and breaks his wand. He has brought about a new level of integration around him and within him. Redefining his relationship with Caliban ("this thing of darkness I / acknowledge mine") is the last thing he does.

Every pair of siblings in the play has both a damaged and a more intact member, and exemplifies the destructive undercurrents of these relationships at their most extreme. Twelve years before the play takes place, Antonio usurped his scholarly, inattentive brother's throne and cast him and his young child out to sea; Prospero repudiates their kinship ("to call [him] brother would even infect my mouth"), although he ultimately forgives him. During their stay on the island, Antonio encourages one of his shipmates, the king of Naples's brother, to plot another fratricide. In both cases the envy and malice of the less successful sibling cause him to wrest power from his brother and make himself the center of attention.

More subtle but no less devastating is the symbolic sibling relationship between Miranda and Caliban. By the time we meet them, there is no more possibility of rivalry; the "sister" is a princess and the "brother" is a slave. Their roles are fixed, and the barriers to mutual affection or empathy unbreachable. Prospero calls her "mine loved darling" and "a third of mine own life" but has only curses for the "demi-devil" Caliban. The radiant beauty and the vicious brute are complete opposites, even in the meaning of their names; his is a near-anagram of "cannibal," and hers means "wonderful." Prospero tells Miranda that he adopted Caliban and at first tried to educate this bastard son of a witch but repudiated the creature—it is never clear whether he is fully human—after he tried to rape her. His opinion and treatment of the repulsive and irredeemable Caliban, whom he keeps enslaved by casting spells that torture him, seem entirely justified:

> *Thou poisonous slave,*
> *Got by the devil himself upon thy wicked*
> *Dam . . .*
> *A devil, a born devil, on whose nature*
> *Nurture can never stick, on whom my pains*
> *Humanely taken, all, all lost, quite lost!*
> *And as with age his body uglier grows,*
> *So his mind cankers.*

Caliban tells a different story. He claims that the attempted rape was an act of vengeance because Prospero had exploited, rejected, and disinherited him:

> *When thou cam'st first,*
> *Thou strok'st me, and made much of me . . .*
> *and then I loved thee*
> *And showed thee all the qualities o'th'isle . . .*
> *Cursed be I that did so. . . .*
> *For I am all the subjects that you have,*
> *Which first was mine own king.*

The education that Prospero so humanely (and perhaps condescendingly) bestowed only increased his frustration and despair:

> *You taught me language, and my profit on't*
> *Is I know how to curse.*

On the surface these two "siblings" are mirror images. But it seems inconsistent that sweet, innocent Miranda, who has compassion for every living creature, expresses nothing but loathing and contempt for Caliban ("'Tis a villain, sir, / I do not love to look on"). She witnesses Prospero torturing him and never protests; in fact, in a speech so cold that many editors believe it to be falsely attributed to her, she justifies and encourages her father's behavior:

> Abhorred slave,
> Which any print of goodness wilt not take,
> Being capable of all ill . . .
> But thy vile race (Though thou didst learn) had that in't which good natures
> Could not abide to be with; therefore wast thou
> Deservedly confined into this rock,
> Who hadst deserved more than a prison.

Just as Miranda's character is imperfectly perfect, Caliban's is not entirely base or dull-witted. Although he certainly does behave monstrously by inciting two drunks to try to kill his master, there is also disturbing evidence that calls into question Prospero's and Miranda's assumptions about him. Caliban speaks some of the most intoxicating poetry in the play:

> Be not afeard, the isle is full of noises,
> Sounds, and sweet airs, that give delight and hurt not;
> Sometimes a thousand twangling instruments
> Will hum about mine ears; and sometime voices,
> That if I then had waked after long sleep,
> Will make me sleep again; and then in dreaming,
> The clouds methought would open, and show riches
> Ready to drop upon me, that when I waked,
> I cried to dream again.

Since the island is his birthright, he has a legitimate grievance. He is a lonely and repulsive outcast whom everyone guiltlessly hurts and humiliates; his bitter hatred is not entirely unjustified. At the end he shows remorse, shame for his terrible judgment, and sincere desire to reform:

> and I'll be wise hereafter,
> And seek for grace. What a thrice-double ass
> Was I to take this drunkard for a god
> and worship this dull fool!

—thereby belying the Prospero family myth that he cannot learn and cannot respond to kindness. Caliban, condemned as inherently and willfully vicious, strives for sense and virtue. He is the only character Prospero underestimates.

Every member of this family is damaged, overtly or covertly; Ariel, the magic spirit who does Prospero's bidding, is spared only because he is not human. No one is exempt from the consequences of being related to Caliban—neither the disillusioned father who repudiates him because of his deformity and rebelliousness, nor the naïve daughter whom Prospero idealizes and makes the bearer of his destiny.

As is typical of parents in these families, Prospero unconsciously repeats with his "son" his traumatic relationship with his own brother when he usurps Caliban's "kingdom" and robs him of his freedom. His own behavior and history shape Caliban's character more than he knows. To label Caliban, whom Prospero sadistically punishes for disobedience, "my slave, who never / Yields us kind answer" is to deny that he has had any role in making his son hate him; why should a slave respond otherwise? Prospero disinherits him and blames Caliban's mother for his physical and mental defects ("This misshapen knave, / His mother was a witch"). He abandons his son, abdicates all responsibility, and then justifies this behavior as deserved and caused exclusively by his son's nature.

> *Since he has defined Caliban as a "beast," Prospero need not treat him humanely:*
> > *Thou most lying slave,*
> *Whom stripes [i.e., lashes] may move, not kindness*

He expresses in extreme terms the buried feelings of a father overwhelmed, as mine was, by an unmanageable disturbed child whom he experiences as alien; dissociating oneself from such a child assuages shame and guilt. Never imagining that his own pedagogic methods could be at fault, this utterly unempathic father insists that his son could not be taught: I did not fail you, you were impossible. He finds a far more appealing and tractable pupil in his daughter. As children do, Caliban lives out the role his family assigns to him. He lashes out at both Prospero and Miranda by assaulting her (as my own brother did in my dream); when one child is perniciously preferred over another—either a damaged or an intact child can be so favored—their relationship is poisoned forever.

Widowed, exiled, and dreadfully disappointed with his son and with his own situation, Prospero turns to his daughter to compensate him for his losses, lavishing all his love and learning upon her; as a woman, she is no threat to his authority. He creates her in his own image and arranges for her to fall in love with a man he chooses, who also adores and idealizes her. He sets her up for life.

Curiously Prospero fails to protect Miranda from Caliban, despite showing the most extreme preference for her; even though

Caliban has tried to rape her, her father insists over her objections that she accompany him to "visit" Caliban. Parents are compelled to expose their intact children to a damaged sibling's outrageous or frightening behavior in order to reinforce their own denial that anything is wrong with the family. Higher-functioning children frequently become embittered and estranged because their parents failed to acknowledge or protect them from a sibling's outbursts. Alternatively, they can join their parents in minimizing the severity of the impact of the exposure and blame themselves for being affected by it. Children who, like Miranda and me, are completely identified with their parents do not register the hostility latent in their parents' treatment of them.

Caliban handles the mental as well as the physical dirty work for the family, as marginalized siblings often do. Prospero recognizes his essential functions:

> But as 'tis,
> We cannot miss [i.e., do without] him. He does make our fire,
> Fetch in our wood, and serves in offices
> That profit us.

His most important "office" is to be defined as the source of all discord and to serve as the repository of all negative emotions—rage, envy, and lust. Caliban embodies the antithesis of Miranda's virtues and makes them gleam even brighter in comparison. His presence is essential because he permits father and daughter to maintain their idyllic, unambivalent bond. Miranda subtly colludes in reinforcing Caliban's role by allying herself exclusively with Prospero's point of view. Her disputed speech accurately expresses the taboo feelings of an intact child; if he is all bad, she can be all good. She validates the legitimacy of her father's actions, insuring her position as the child who is no trouble, a source only of delight, inspiration, and joy: Miranda needs Caliban in order to be Miranda.

Splitting character traits between siblings is common in damaged families, and it is only a superficial advantage for the one who is assigned the positive characteristics. A person who defines herself in opposition to another can never develop an independent identity and is always warding off the dark side the other represents. The task of every intact sibling is to recognize this split and reabsorb the qualities that she has colluded in depositing in her opposite.

Caliban symbolizes not only Miranda's damaged sibling but also Prospero's, as well as everything in his own character that he disavows. Coming to terms with him is Prospero's final and most difficult achievement. He anticipates their confrontation with more trepidation and outrage than his reunion with his brother Antonio, whose treachery had less justification. "We must prepare to meet with Caliban," he grimly tells Ariel (not wanting to face his nemesis alone), as the hour of the planned conspiracy approaches, even though he has arranged for it to fail. Miranda remarks, "Never till this day / Saw I him touched with anger, so distempered." Meeting Caliban arouses such intense emotions because it is Prospero's ultimate encounter with himself.

After Prospero gives up his magic powers and forgives his brother, he directs Ariel to catch Caliban and his confederates and to terrify and befoul them. When they appear before his entourage suitably chastised, he says:

> *this thing of darkness I*
> *Acknowledge mine . . .*
> *He is as disproportioned in his manners*
> *As in his shape. Go, sirrah, to my cell:*
> *. . . As you look*
> *To have my pardon, trim it handsomely.*

Caliban responds:

> *Ay, that I will; and I'll be wise hereafter,*
> *And seek for grace.*

In this exchange the relationship between Prospero and Caliban is transformed. Caliban is no longer Prospero's slave but his willing servant. Prospero becomes a different kind of master, one who motivates not with the threat of punishment but with the promise of forgiveness. Caliban voluntarily and remorsefully accepts the task of cleaning Prospero's quarters. They are left together at the end, their bond now based on choice rather than compulsion.

But since Shakespeare is a realist, this is not an unambivalent resolution. They accept but do not love one another; there is no sentimental embrace—although they did shake hands in one misguided production I saw. Their inequities of station do not vanish; Prospero cannot resist calling attention to Caliban's deformity and illegitimacy and continues to order him around. The servant is still sullen and uncouth, and the master has not stopped being arrogant and superior. Caliban remains a thing of darkness, but now he is an acknowledged one. There can never be "closure" in their relationship, only expanded possibilities. Yet Caliban acquires humanity, and Prospero regains it. Their rapprochement, partial yet profound, is a model of how an intact sibling can begin to integrate a damaged one.

The order of events in the play's denouement is psychologically significant; Prospero must renounce magic and pardon his brother before he can acknowledge Caliban. First he gives up the illusion of omnipotence, the self-righteous conviction that he is unrelated to Caliban and that he can keep himself separate and untainted forever. Accepting his own past and his troubled relationship with his brother Antonio is also a necessary prerequisite. Coming to terms with Caliban—who, like all siblings and sons, inhabits Prospero's internal as well as external world—is the final step in ending his isolation and reentering society as a more fully developed man.

Miranda is the only member of the "family" who does not change, because she never acknowledges her kinship with Caliban; their relationship simply ends when she leaves to marry the man her father chose for her and to become queen of Naples. She never questions her judgment of him even when she has been proved wrong. She is so intoxicated with her beloved and with the opportunity to continue her seemingly perfect life that she hardly notices the changes around her. Real Mirandas cannot go away and find unambivalent love without consequences, however hard they may try. Because coming to terms with Caliban is coming into one's own, the price of avoidance and flight is to stay a dutiful daughter/ wife forever and never to evolve into a fully independent, self-aware woman; without her shadow she has no depth—and without compassion for Caliban, she can never have true compassion for herself.

What will become of Caliban? His fate and future relationship to Prospero are uncertain; reconnecting is all that matters. Such relationships have built-in conflicts that never cease and do not need to. By the end Prospero has lost Miranda, but he keeps Caliban. Will he take him back as a servant to Milan? Will he give him back the island? He does not free him as he does Ariel because Ariel is an aspect of his magic, not of his human nature. Prospero, and his audience, can never be free of Caliban. He is part of all of us. If we become wiser and recognize our humanity, we too can change our relationship with him, though we cannot sever it.

chapter 4

America's Damaged Families

IN THE REAL WORLD as in the dramatic world of *The Tempest*, nobody in a family is exempt from the chronic crisis that a damaged child creates. Though few parents respond as disastrously as Prospero does, stress permeates even the most loving household. The personalities of the parents and their own histories determine how they deal with the trauma and whether they turn their children into Calibans and Mirandas. Only the wisest and most emotionally fortunate avoid imposing massive portions of their own old conflicts upon them. Whatever the family dynamic ends up being, the normal child will be scarred, even if the scars do not show.

It is hard to imagine the level of tumult, anxiety, and sheer effort that life in a damaged family involves. The abnormal is nor-mal; siblings who return home after a respite are shocked at the intensity of the distress they endured every day—the retarded brother's blasting radio at six A.M., the autistic sister's tantrum over a lost purple crayon—that they now realize they minimized in order to endure. They bear an inner weight of unarticulated sorrow at having missed much of the freedom and insouciance of child-hood that others take for granted. "I spent summers playing in the hallways at the Mayo Clinic during my sister's surgeries when other kids thought mayo was something you spread on bread," a minister recalled wistfully. The injury need not be catastrophic for a problem sibling to loom larger than a normal one; you still have to, in the words of an anorectic woman's sister, "arrange life around it."

To discover that a child is seriously impaired in mind or body changes everything. Whether the news comes at birth or later—and even if the extent of the problem is unknown or ignored—it plunges parents into mourning and casts a pall over their lives. Overtly or covertly their initial despair gets communicated to their other children. It is shattering to realize that you will be denied for-ever the very satisfactions for which people have children in the first place, that your gratifications will be limited and your responsibili-ties and anxieties ever-expanding. You worry about providing proper care your whole life and about who will take over after your death. This is the gravest possible blow to the universal fantasy that a child will be a perfected version of oneself, that family life will be harmonious, and that siblings will unambivalently love one another.

Even when parents eventually accept their fate and find mean-ing in whatever relationship is possible with the child, disappointment and the loss of possibility are permanent, revived whenever they witness the rituals and achievements of ordinary life—the graduations, weddings, and professional successes—that other parents savor. Family members are forever adjusting expectations, trying to make the best of it. Healthy children notice and cannot be protected from the truth. They grieve, they feel guilty, and they struggle to compensate by achieving for two.

What families learn about a child's disability and when they learn it affects how they respond. Immediate despair that a baby has been born with cerebral palsy is different from the slowly dawning distress that a first-grader who looks normal cannot learn to read or the uncomprehending, helpless horror of watching a seemingly healthy adolescent slip into madness. No wonder parents minimize the problems when they can, hoping against hope that their child is only "different," "sensitive," or a "late bloomer." Nobody can help covertly comparing the problem child to all the perfectly healthy ones in the neighborhood; a nurse whose multiply handicapped sister was her parents' full-time project and her own after-school responsibility recalled envying the happy, normal family of ten next door.

Many siblings never even know a sibling's diagnosis, either because the condition is hard to categorize or because the parents choose not to find out. Ambiguity heightens their anxiety, and they grow up with an undercurrent of vague depression and nameless dread that must be kept to themselves. They learn to keep secrets.

Abnormal children provoke forbidden feelings that are too painful and shocking for most parents to admit; wanting to abandon one's own flesh and blood, hoping they will die, wishing they had never been born, repulsion—and even hatred—are utterly antithetical to what good people are supposed to feel. Adoptive parents are troubled by thoughts of wanting to give the child back. Every parent lives with ambivalence, but theirs is not sufficiently offset by joy. Destructive fantasies are more dangerous because they would be easier, and more tempting, to carry out against a helpless, troublesome child. A headhunter I interviewed with a cerebral palsied brother had no trouble identifying with Richard and Dawn Kelso, the philanthropic couple active in advocacy for the disabled who made headlines in December 1999 by wheeling their afflicted ten-year-old son into an emergency room once too often and leaving him there. Unless religious parents consider their fate a manifestation of God's will or a mark of divine favor, they bear the additional burden of feeling like sinners as well as victims. A sense of shame and defectiveness ("How could I produce a Caliban?") alternates with a desire to blame the child or the other parent, as Prospero does. Putting feelings aside in order to do one's duty consumes less energy than facing the full brunt of a tragic predicament.

Caretakers who cannot accept their terrible thoughts must bend over backward to prove they care; obsessive dedication to the disabled neutralizes the desire to neglect or destroy them. They throw themselves into the problem, or they throw the problem away by denying how bad it is—often at the cost of their relationships with their spouse and their other children. Problem children hold together many a bad marriage and destroy many a good one. What parents cannot allow themselves to feel, they cannot allow their normal children to feel either; any uncensored emotional outburst ("Can't we send Johnny to Mars or just not bring him home from camp?") would hold up a mirror to what they struggle to excise in themselves. The cycle of guilt, denial, and expiation, of alternating overcompensation and avoidance, inevitably draws the normal child in. Like a barely detectable sound or smell, unmentionable, unmetabolized pain pervades the atmosphere.

To recognize that guilt over violent wishes plagues all intact family members does not detract from their genuine devotion; confronting and learning to tolerate hostility makes authentic compassion for oneself as well as for the afflicted possible. Labeling and accepting taboo emotions defangs them. Insight protects the healthy from compulsion, frees them from self-torture, and enhances their efforts on behalf of their abnormal relatives; facing hatred deepens love.

Contrary to appearances, parents' emotional needs, not their children's, determine whether a Caliban (or a she-Caliban) is designated as central or peripheral in a family. What these children evoke from their parents' own family experience—particularly unresolved issues with siblings—influences how they are treated more than the type or severity of their injuries. Two families in which the damaged children have identical diagnoses can be radically different to grow up in. The memories, fantasies, ideals, and fears of the parents create the template into which a child's actual personality is fit—the more unresolved the conflicts, the more procrustean the template. Gender also matters; fathers may bury themselves in work, and mothers in overinvolvement with the difficult child. If, like Prospero, a father who had a brutal rivalry with a brother cannot bear his own sense of failure and disappointment, he will reject or ignore his impaired son and focus all his attention on his normal daughter, adoring her but also demanding perfection and obedience from her, obliterating her difficulties and failing to protect her from her brother's outbursts. Likewise, a mother who feels inferior to her sister may find a vocation in dedicating her life to a disabled daughter while simultaneously belittling, rebuking, and neglecting her normal one and pressing her into service as her auxiliary in life and her surrogate thereafter. Self-sacrifice masks retroactive revenge—she punishes her sister by favoring the daughter who reminds her of herself.

Even in wealthy families sustained contact with siblings, no matter how seriously dysfunctional, is regarded as a duty, just as it is on *The Tempest*'s desert isle; the motivation is emotional, not financial. Adults who embrace caretaking with a vengeance typically expect their unimpaired children (especially daughters) to follow suit and subtly communicate that to demur is unconscionable. Younger girls frequently baby-sit for and physically tend their older brothers and sisters at the expense of their own social lives, their roles a combination of precocious parents and unpaid practical nurses. A woman with a brain-damaged brother remembered that "Rita, help us out" was a constant refrain in her house. Healthy siblings get involuntarily elected "family vice-presidents,"* with responsibilities but no authority.

Problem children get away with murder because their parents practice a covert form of favoritism, the disciplinary double standard. They are treated with a confusing combination of authoritarianism and overindulgence, while a far stricter code of conduct applies to the healthy child, who must not have or be any problem. Rivalry between normal and handicapped children is particularly

---

*Z. Stoneman and P. Berman, eds. *The Effects of Mental Retardation, Disability and Illness on Sibling Relationships: Research Issues and Challenges* (Baltimore: Paul H. Brookes, 1993), p. 357.

hard for parents to tolerate. Discouraging competition drives animosity underground, where it festers.

A young painter torn between pursuing her art on one coast and taking up the role of her brain-damaged brother's guardian on the other described her predicament:

> It's a tremendous burden that my brother has a head injury. I'm supposed to be Mother Teresa—you're put in position and expected to make something great of it—you're always grieving that there's nothing you can do to save the situation. My parents never let themselves get upset. My father looks down on my brother and doesn't interact with him. My mother doesn't stand up to him and tell him he can't manipulate us all by having temper tantrums. I'm the receptacle of everybody's feelings.

Healthy children in damaged households get too much attention or too little but rarely enough of the right kind. If resources are concentrated on rehabilitating and managing the problem child, they become invisible; or if, like Miranda, they are chosen to repair their parents' broken dreams, they become vessels of exaggerated expectations. Some are actually conceived as replacements to compensate for their parents' disappointments or to provide what one designated sibling bitterly called "genetically engineered caretaking." Either way they are abandoned.

How can hurt feelings or a skinned knee ever take precedence over the trials of a sibling who is paraplegic or paranoid? Normal children—even preferred ones—never come first in a crisis and must stifle the impulse to object. One attention-starved little girl begged to be enrolled in the same school for the neurologically impaired that her brother attended, but her parents still did not get the message. Research shows that intact children—and also their seriously impaired siblings—thrive when the dysfunctional sibling is finally institutionalized because they are relieved of constantly having to accommodate the other's difficulties and deformities. Finally they can bring a friend or a date home without dread.

Even outside the family nobody—including researchers on disability—notices normal ones. One study examined the effects of sibling kidney transplants on recipients but ignored donors. Another analyzed how vision-impaired children fared with sighted sibling guides without considering the feelings of the guides. When it comes to sibling dynamics, psychologists are as blind as their subjects.

Problem children frequently require disproportionate amounts of attention from their parents, and normal siblings are inevitably neglected. But many parents allow the abnormal one to deplete the oxygen of family life by imagining—and communicating—that the normal one is low-maintenance. Not only do healthy children get less care; they are assumed to need less. Parental justifications and expectations—subjective interpretations rather than objective needs—do the deepest damage. When a successful lawyer whose brother had made repeated suicide attempts announced to his mother that he was getting a divorce, she said, "You were supposed to be my happy child." Another mother told her daughter by way of encouragement, "Isn't it great that you're okay, so you can take care of yourself?" Parental neglect is also fostered by envy; the normal child did not produce the "monster" and is not responsible for its problems—and one day he can escape.

Since their children's dark emotions are even more threatening than their own, parents implicitly pressure them never to express—or even to recognize—rage, terror, or resentment. Split-off feelings do more damage because they cannot be integrated, and they influence behavior in ways the person cannot see.

Love and fear cause children to don their parents' emotional straitjackets. They want to identify, show solidarity, and provide consolation; they need to avoid stigma, secure their own position in the family, and guarantee their parents' love. "My parents never admitted that they were depressed or angry, so my anger was strangled too," said the sister of a hyperactive woman who could not speak. "There are the taboo things you can never say, like 'I wish you never existed,' that you would tell a normal sister and never think twice." Thinking, acting, and feeling only what you are supposed to becomes another type of caretaking. The best way to prove to others and to reassure yourself that you are different from a damaged sibling is to have no difficulties, make no demands, and harbor no grudges; to be perfect and prematurely mature are universal signs of the Caliban Syndrome. Your mission is to become the mirror image of the damaged sibling whose likeness threatens to emerge at any time—and that always will.

Every intact sibling secretly wonders, "Why didn't it happen to me—or when will it?"—the fear of contagion that is an earmark of the Caliban Syndrome. Sharing a sibling's awful fate would be fitting punishment for the guilty triumph of being better off; survivor guilt plagues every normal one, overtly or covertly. Dreams about the damaged one dying or being cured are common; both solutions make the problem vanish.

An "invisible fence" like those used to keep dogs in yards cordons off the dangerous emotions of normal children. A dog is shocked for straying and learns to confine itself to designated boundaries. Eventually external constraints are unnecessary. Nothing shows; the dog seems miraculously tractable. In the psyches of healthy siblings, the all-too-human anxiety and hostility disappear like the natural canine impulse to chase cars.

In an ingenious study, a researcher had two small and overtly well-adjusted children improvise a "radio play" about their mute brother. Her tape recordings revealed extraordinarily intense fantasies of murder, mutilation, decapitation, and torture "not readily visible in their lives."*

The inner world of normal siblings brims with secrets, hidden from themselves as much as from others. All their lives they seek a sanctuary untouched by the other's plight, a door they can close without guilt. Everybody tells them they are the lucky ones; what right have they to complain? Their lonely sorrow is as intolerable as their sadism. Fulfilling such stringent expectations of being good, responsible, and trouble-free is a full-time job that leaves little time for living.

As adults, competent siblings may not be intimates, but at least they are equals. A damaged brother or sister will never be a peer, a companion, or a confidant. If the younger sibling is the normal one, role reversal begins at birth; a young athlete remembers painstakingly trying to teach his spastic older brother to ride a bicycle. The most tender bond with a caretaker or advocate cannot be fully reciprocal. Even when someone says, "My Down syndrome sister taught me the true meaning of love," there are unacknowledged losses in that love.

---

*Helen Featherstone, *A Difference in the Family: Living with a Disabled Child* (New York: Penguin, 1981), p. 35.

*   *   *

MEDIA COVERAGE of the troubled and disabled, with its relentless tone of moral uplift, sanctifies every stricture families impose on their normal siblings. The topic seems to evoke nothing but treacly sentimentality. ("My retarded sister is my hero—my love, my heart, my angel," a movie star told *Us* magazine.) The press recognizes only one role for them: members of the "starting lineup of a team deep in talent," as the usually restrained *New York Times* called the brother and sister of the first quadriplegic to graduate from Harvard. Like a Homeric epithet, "supportive" always precedes their names.

Uncritically extolling self-effacement as their natural and proper vocation undermines normal children's right to dreams of their own. Helping the mentally or physically handicapped is always presented as a family project; to participate with less than wholehearted enthusiasm is unthinkable. The Harvard graduate's "teammates" have already tolerated their mother attending classes with their paralyzed sister since she was eight and leaving the family in another state to live in her dormitory room through college. Now they are expected to bask in her reflected glory for the rest of their lives. They are supposed to accept altruistically that, even if they too were to graduate from Harvard, there would be no front-page photograph of their mother walking triumphantly beside them, no heartwarming TV special, no book contract or motivational speaking career; being their sister's sibling forever defines and confines them.

There is a troubling undercurrent in stories like this: that narcissism can lurk beneath the veneer of maternal devotion, and that obsessive dedication to one child, however deserving, can lead to the abandonment of others, who have no choice but to participate in their mother's herculean efforts.

Even the neurologist Oliver Sacks perpetuates the myth of the saintly sibling. In an article* about an autistic painter whose parents—both professors—devoted their lives to scrutinizing her symptomatology and wrote two books minutely detailing her development, he mentions in passing her "intellectually gifted and accomplished" brothers and sisters. The household is "one where eager interest and attention turn in all directions, and where intellectual play and fun pervade the atmosphere." Seduced by this idyllic fantasy, he does not imagine that these children could harbor any resentment of their parents' extraordinary preoccupation with their deeply troubled sister or that living with her might not have been an unalloyed delight.

The saddest consequence of the inspirational imperative is that many normal siblings buy into it. Finding no corrective in the culture to the role in which their families cast them, they embrace it with zeal. When, in a departure from the norm, *The New York Times* published a story on the tribulations of siblings of the disabled, one wrote an immediate disclaimer in a letter to the editor, insisting that growing up with a retarded sister had caused her no difficulty whatsoever.

Any account of the triumphs of the disabled that ignores the toll on their siblings—even if the siblings themselves collude in denying that toll—is naïve at best and irresponsible at worst. It is, however, an easy trap to fall into. In *My Left Foot*, the bracingly

*Oliver Sacks, "Leaving Nirvana," *New York Review of Books*, March 31, 2001.

uncloying film about a paralyzed Irish artist, there is a scene in which the hero's father and brood of siblings grumble that their mother has once again served them nothing but watered-down oatmeal at tea because she spends what little money there is for his rehabilitation. I never gave a thought to the impact on them until I began researching this book.

While some siblings accept, and even embrace, their destiny as members of the "team," others are (mostly privately) outraged, having experienced the obverse of the soothing stereotype in their own families. A graphic designer whose autistic brother tried to strangle her when they were children, and who struggled for years to get her parents to recognize the danger he presented, is acutely aware of the discrepancy between the illusion and the reality of damaged families:

> I'm trying to eradicate the *Hallmark Hall of Fame Special* myth—"how I learned the meaning of life by having a disabled sibling." The cover of *Newsweek* on autism had a beautiful blond good boy. People just want to look at the pretty kids on *Jerry Lewis*, the sanitized version, not the ugly cases like my brother. The severely disabled aren't telegenic. It's a crisis when elderly caregivers die—siblings should not be expected to sacrifice their lives. I would have killed myself or both of us if I'd been forced to take my brother in—it shouldn't have to be a choice between my life and his. Too bad if I don't want to go into special ed as my profession—who signed me up?

Normal siblings have two life tasks: to recognize the enormous impact a damaged sibling has on them, and to forge an identity in which that sibling is peripheral. The first makes the second possible.

My Sister Ate My Homework

At Home with Damaged Siblings

EIGHT-YEAR-OLD JACKIE HANSON spent hours putting the finishing touches on the cover of her very first book report—crayons, sequins, glitter, the works. But her pride was short-lived, and her teacher never saw her resplendent creation. She had to hand in her assignment the next day with no cover—and no explanation—at all. Thinking it might be tasty, her autistic sister had ripped the cover off and chewed it up when Jackie wasn't looking. "I couldn't be angry—how could I be?—when she messed up like that," Jackie recalled. "Ambivalent feelings weren't allowed, only love and strength."

Incidents like this are commonplace when you grow up with an abnormal sibling, even one whose difficulties are less catastrophic than Jackie's sister's. A far cry from the petty squabbles of the "he hit me"/ "he hit me first" variety, the onslaughts are relentless, pervasive, and extreme—and so traumatic that healthy siblings' voices quiver when recounting them years later: "A simple conversation was nails on a blackboard"; "We lived in a state of siege"; "It doesn't have the cachet, but it's just as painful as a mother dying of cancer"; "I always think that people with normal siblings seem so foreign—how could it be possible?" they say. That so many of them suppressed their true feelings at the time is part of the trauma of the Caliban Syndrome.

Unlike the usual sibling conflicts, these problems rarely diminish when you leave home, and they often escalate. And what happens when your parents die? Violations great and small disrupt childhood, complicate adolescence, cast a pall over adulthood, and loom much larger than typical troubles with brothers and sisters, even if the culprit dies. A minister developed hypertension and suffered anxiety attacks after her deformed and retarded sister died. A man in his seventies still vividly recalls his sister's scenes at age six. As a hospital administrator who was beginning to process the impact that her brother's tragic combination of explosiveness, dedicated scholarship, and ultimately fatal muscular dystrophy had on her life declared, "Once a sibling, always a sibling."

Home life is a series of little murders of privacy, pleasure, peace of mind. Beloved possessions get ruined without repercussions—the carefully constructed train display wrecked, the prom dress bought with a hard-earned paycheck hung back in the closet besmirched with pizza. Either because they could not understand or are exempted by parents, the culprits are rarely punished. Family activities get spoiled. "We never went to church or a movie together because somebody always had to stay with her," said a veterinarian whose multiply handicapped sister "could not be left alone for a second." A violent, neurologically impaired boy's sister remembered how "everything focused on him—which house we lived in, what TV shows we watched. We catered to him completely at home because his life sucked."

An actor's parents never attended any of his high school performances because they had no one to watch their reclusive daughter. A painter, on the other hand, wished her parents had not attended her piano recital; they brought along her furious brain-injured brother, who, just as she sat down to play, shouted out, "You're not my sister—you're some stranger!" for the entire audience to hear. A nurse's parents permitted her "completely nutty" learning-disabled brother to drag the whole family to twenty-six stores to find him the right pair of shoes. One teenager discovered that her brain-damaged brother was calling her friends up for dates in the middle of the night, and another that his alcoholic sister went knocking on his friends' doors. A retarded boy and a learning-disabled girl bombarded their normal sister from both directions: "You couldn't say a sentence without one or the other interrupting, and you could never have anything last." The normal ones were all expected to endure these trials with the patience and adult understanding—the premature maturity—that no child naturally possesses.

Social life suffers drastically. Many such children curtail activities to baby-sit for siblings, often much older than they, when paid caretakers are unwilling or unaffordable. And who wants to have

71

friends over when your sister parades around in her underwear, or jumps out and rips people's clothes, or when your unwashed, belching brother punches people to say hello? An obese, peculiar, or anti-social sibling also makes you look bad in the eyes of the all-important peer group. "I could never bear to tell my friends that my sister took the 'retard bus' to school," a magazine editor recalled, fearing that her sister's deficiency would somehow reflect badly on her although she was a superb student herself. Naturally the healthy children try to flee or pretend their nemesis does not exist.

But going out is as excruciating as staying in. A minister's daughter remembers hiding under the pew at church when she was supposed to sing hymns to avoid being associated with her autistic sister. A political scientist's brother with Tourette's syndrome and autism "mortified" him, and his own "inhumane" response haunts him still:

> There was a high threshold of people I wouldn't bring home or tell. I felt such shame—it was a constant internal struggle. I just couldn't stand being seen in public with him and wanted to hide under a rock, and now I want to suppress those feelings. I want to slug people who snicker as much as I want to back away myself. Sometimes I long to put my arms around him and stare down anybody giggling, to stand between him and others to shield them or him. Every time I step outside, I'm repelled by him and repelled by my repulsion.

Defending a damaged sibling from the scorn of strangers expresses compassion while simultaneously assuaging guilt for secretly sharing their prejudices. While some people look back on their earlier embarrassment and judge it selfish, "spoiled bratty," or worse ("I feel I'm evil because I still want to run away from her and try to find ways to escape dealing with her"), for many their childhood dread of how their playmates would react evolves into adult dread of how fiancés, colleagues, and utter strangers will react. ("When people ask if you have a brother and what does he do, I try to change the subject—I'm so glad I live out of town," the political scientist said.) When a lawyer's drunken, paranoid brother came banging on her office door, her first response was not fear but relief that no clients or colleagues were around to witness it. A Caliban is a terrible reflection on you and, on the deepest level, of you as well.

Normal siblings are inundated daily with behavior that is not only noxious but also frightening, incomprehensible, and wretchedly sad. Pity and outrage intermingle, and anger implodes, when the perpetrator is also a victim. A novelist whose disturbed older brother endured both ostracism and multiple eye operations, and beat her up with impunity, described her complicated reactions: "He was such an outcast—so isolated, such an ugly, weird kid and so abysmally lonely that I knew he was hurting all the time. That he was both sick and vicious made it extremely confusing." "I was forbidden from being mean to him, and he could be mean to me— when he got taunted, I became his punching bag," said Jennifer Martin, the hospital administrator whose perpetually enraged brother had a fatal form of muscular dystrophy. "But how could you wish someone would die who was going to die?" Wrestling alone with such devastating contradictions drives some to consider suicide and others to run away from home.

The hardest thing to tolerate is the inevitable but unpredictable temper tantrums to which siblings across the entire spectrum of difficulties are prone. You know their frustrated anguish will cause an eruption, but you never know what will provoke it or when. Most parents handle this situation abysmally, permitting the abnormal child to become a tyrant and demanding forbearance from the more rational one. "My mother's line was always 'She's not well, so you should give in to her so she won't throw a tantrum,'" said a financial adviser of her explosive borderline sister. "Her agonies took precedence." "I was told as a kid 'Be nice to your poor sister,'" a boutique owner said. "There was always an excuse for her outbursts, and I had to dance around them. She used up the family quota on scenes."

Many people use the metaphor of a "time bomb" to describe the chronic, palpable tension they lived with. Anxiety hangs over the dinner table, follows you into the car on outings, and punctuates weekends; there are no respites. An artist said of her brain-damaged brother, "You didn't even have to pull the cord very hard, and there's no real reason when it goes off. I could never let my guard down. I had to be mobilized—there was such an undercurrent of anger that he could direct at you." The memories persist years afterward; "he has tantrums in my dreams—they're indelible."

Some injuries are so incapacitating that one woman described living with her afflicted sister as "like having a dog around"—but even dogs can be taught to behave. Compassion wears thin when neither the sibling nor the parents make any attempt at control. Illness or disability evokes passionate determination and self-reliance in some people and sullen self-involvement in others. A retarded brother is "selfish, not just slow—he blasts his music all night because he's angry inside," said the brother who had to listen to it. A neurologically impaired brother leaves all chores to his able-bodied sister: "I'm frustrated with him for being lazy and never helping—even if it's his brain, can't he try? If I tell him, he gets furious. Underneath I don't believe it's all the disability; I think he's mad at the world and at me," she concluded. Parents frequently do not intervene, set proper limits, or defend their normal children's rights. Self-indulgence and disregard erode sympathy when the acting out never stops. After getting the tenth call from the police, "I hold her at least partly responsible," said a manic-depressive's sister. "She's thirty-seven and has been given options, but she plays the mental illness card whenever it suits her."

Normal children also absorb an inordinate amount of their parents' stress. Seeing your mother weeping in the kitchen from exhaustion every night after striving all day to find the right placement for your multihandicapped sister who never seems to fit the treatment criteria ("the deaf schools won't accept her because she's blind, and the retarded programs say she's too high-functioning") takes a silent toll, making the witness feel simultaneously helpless and hyperresponsible. Misplaced parental anxiety has overt consequences as well; a stockbroker remembers that, after his eighteen-year-old sister was arrested for selling heroin, his father, fearing that he would be corrupted by the same bad company, precipitously moved the family to another town and sent him away to boarding school.

Parents can go to shocking lengths to shield a damaged child, irreparably harming the normal one in the process. "My sister wet her bed until age fourteen. Our mother took off her wet sheets and put them on my bed so the maid wouldn't think badly of her," the financial adviser recalled. A television producer who shared a bed with her enuretic retarded sister at times during their childhoods (although the family was not destitute) remembers the urine flowing to her side of the bed, literally immersing her in her sister's physicality. In a dream the sister of an autistic boy graphically portrayed the unacknowledged damage he inflicted:

> I realize that my brother has been missing the toilet for years, and that the eaves of the house are dripping with his urine. When I point this out to my mother, she replies nonchalantly, "It's an act of God."

"Take Susie along" is an oft-repeated refrain. Children are entreated by their frantic parents to include abnormal siblings of all sorts in their activities and to share their friends, which they are often loath to do. The distinction between loving inclusion and guilty coercion gets blurred. "I couldn't have my own life," says an architect who was pressured to invite her bizarre brother to her sweet-sixteen party. The parents may insist on taking Susie along themselves; a gifted student's mother and father made her tour of prospective colleges a family affair and brought along her hyperactive brother, who ran away and was found hours later by the police. Sometimes you have to go along with Susie against your will; a teacher was sent to the same camp as her partially blind, depressed sister. "I loved it, but she hated it because she couldn't make friends, so our parents came and took us both home." As a teenager, the veterinarian with the severely disabled sister spent her summers working as a counselor at a camp for the handicapped at her parents' behest—a job that she expected her own children, all normal, to take on. The demands parents make on a normal one are frequently passed along to posterity.

Feeling obligated to make these siblings more central than you want, and feeling resentful or wretched about not wanting to, does not stop when you no longer live together; you agonize about their role on significant occasions for the rest of your life. "I'm already worrying about having to spend Christmas with her and her horrible passive husband after my mother dies, and my mother's in perfect health," the sister of a troubled narcissist observed. A designer spent most of her own baby shower trying to coax her bulimic sister out of the bathroom where she had locked herself, and the financial adviser's borderline sister has not spoken to her for forty years because she made someone else her maid of honor. They steel themselves for their parents' funerals.

Distance lends perspective—and disenchantment—to what you endured at home and unwittingly adapted to. Every time actor Jack Morelli enters the house where his family still lives, the poignancy of his reclusive sister's life hits him afresh. "I get caught up in how sad it is, how someone can exist like this. I feel like a guest there because everything is so regimented," he said. A teacher with a retarded brother found that "it's really hard going back and seeing how they yell rather than teach him how to do things. Everybody's even more frustrated now because he's older. I forget how it was." "Gosh, I thought he was better than this," said a librarian who minimized the severity of his autistic brother's disability to assuage his own guilt for moving away. More than one normal sibling was disturbed enough by a visit to seek treatment afterward.

Some siblings, like Amy Goodman, a young publicist with a

schizophrenic brother, never dare to go home because they know what awaits them:

> The chance that the homeless person I see on the street in my town could be my own brother scares the shit out of me—this is somebody I grew up with. I don't want to be presented with his illness at its height; if I can avoid that I will.

Despite your best efforts, however, impossible siblings have a way of showing up at your door—or, on one memorable occasion, in the river in front of your door, as happened to Janice Becker:

> My crazy sister went AWOL from the hospital. She came to my apartment, ran down to the Ohio River in her underwear, raving that I was the devil, and jumped in. I got helicopters and police boats, but she's so strong that it took hours to fish her out. The story was on the first page of the local paper—without a picture, thank God.

Lots of people have less than Grandma Moses–perfect holiday family gatherings, but few are as dramatically awful as the one that boutique owner Mimi Newhouse's mother and borderline sister ruined:

> I'd cooked a full Thanksgiving dinner, everybody's there. My sister picks up the tablecloth and proceeds to throw everything off the table, screaming "You're so selfish." Dishes go crashing, the meal's destroyed. The rest of the evening is spent

cleaning up and trying to put something together. Then my mother comes over to me and whispers, "You know she's not all there. She's very sensitive."

The fallout can continue into the next generation. The lawyer's schizophrenic brother not only appeared at her office but made a nutcracker shaped like a penis and insisted on displaying it to her young daughters at her home. "He had no idea it was disturbing, offensive, and appalling," she said, as she struggled to decide whether to bar him from visiting in the future. Not only does the destructive behavior persist, but the parental attitudes that failed to contain it do also. The perverse pattern of preference is repeated, as parents, who are now grandparents, cannot attend their grandchildren's graduations because their multihandicapped daughter is home from the institution for the weekend. A real estate broker said, "I told my mother that I wouldn't bring my son to see her if my sister the drug-addicted prostitute was there, and she said, 'Then I guess you're not coming around anymore.'" When a seriously learning-disabled woman finally married, her sister said, "I hope she doesn't get pregnant right away, because her baby will monopolize our mother's attention just as my sister always did." Their tone is primarily one of resignation, not complaint.

In the midst of adult pursuits—college, child-rearing, making a living—healthy siblings are forced to deal with brothers and sisters in crises ranging from bouncing checks to hijacking jets, from drunken stupors to homicides. The role of rescuer is thrust upon them by siblings, parents, or their own heightened sense of duty. Their feeling of responsibility can be uncompromising; while she was recuperating from chemotherapy, a woman's depressed brother shot himself through the head in their parents' home, and she blamed herself that she did not have the stamina to stop him.

Even a sibling's happiness provokes anxiety. "What if he meets someone in the day care program and gets married?" fretted a retarded man's sister, picturing herself trapped forever taking care of his prospective progeny. She felt she would be forced to choose between his fulfillment and her own all over again.

Nobody simply grows apart from a damaged brother or sister, as do people with functioning siblings whose lives diverge; obligation, guilt, or the need to repudiate are too great. Whether they rebel or comply, their parents' admonition to take care of the troubled one makes them maintain at least minimal contact; an involuntary bond binds them together.

A sibling does not have to be massively incapacitated to weigh you down. You may keep your distance physically, but psychically the clingy, whiny sister on her fourth marriage, and the obnoxious, parasitic brother on his fourth job, lurk in the background, disturbing your peace of mind. "I rarely see her though she lives a few blocks away," advertising executive Dana Thompson said of the fragile older sister she never got along with. "Everything is always about her, even when my son was born and our father was dying. Our mother keeps encouraging us to have a relationship, but I can't stand to spend time with her. She becomes overwrought at the smallest thing and starts screaming at every family occasion. I know she's had a harder life than I have, but she makes no effort, and we have nothing in common. No matter what I give, it's never enough." As we spoke about this troubled and troubling woman, Dana realized how deep her repulsion actually went and how intertwined their destinies continued to be despite her attempts to extricate herself: "She's like a little worm that invades everywhere, a thread that's another color—purple thread in a pink fabric, subtle but there—a nut I can't crack."

SOMETIMES THE "LOVE AND STRENGTH" that Jackie Hanson summoned at age eight when her sister ate her book report cover are bound to fail, and the taboo feelings so carefully suppressed come tumbling out. It happens to most siblings, and it haunts them for the rest of their lives. They never forget these scenes and never forgive themselves for being so human.

Randy Lane looks like a winner in life's lottery. Boyish, athletic, with all-American good looks, he is one of the country's most prominent young political scientists, a tenured professor at age thirty-five. His affability and laid-back charm make it hard to imagine the hidden anguish he still feels because of a night twenty years ago when, provoked beyond endurance by his autistic, Tourette's-afflicted older brother, he lost control:

> I was at my parents' beach house with a bunch of friends from college. He insisted I play a game of Sorry with him—we used to play board games and I'd always let him win—and threw a tantrum when I refused. I couldn't take it anymore, and we started physically fighting in front of everybody. I had my hands on his throat, holding him down, and he screamed at me, "I wish you'd never been born." "Shut up, you fucking faggot," I yelled back. Then I said, "Don't blame me, it's God's

fault." My mother started weeping and promised "we'll never let him embarrass you again," and then drove home with him in the middle of the night. I was devastated by the unfairness and the tragedy, and she thought it was just embarrassment I was feeling. We never discussed it. What I did was disloyal, dishonorable, and unchristian.

Even in his rage the insult Randy hurled at his brother was generic; to have actually repeated back what his brother had said to him would have been unutterable because it was too true. And while he deflected the blame for his brother's miserable condition onto God, he himself still bears the guilt for his momentary lapse of compassion. Like so many normal siblings, the person for whom he really has too little compassion is himself.

chapter 6

My Sister
Spoke to Me

Dreams of Normal
Siblings

AT NIGHT normal ones tell themselves truths about their predicament that no one—themselves included—listens to during the day. Their dreams, which have never been systematically studied before, provide a unique glimpse of a secret world, expressed in poignant and poetic personal language.

The purpose of dreams is to expose the unacknowledged dimensions of experience. Since normal siblings must conceal a salient part of their inner lives from themselves, their dreams are especially telling and are the most unvarnished source of information about the emotions their damaged siblings evoke. During sleep, when their guard is down and the consequences of self-disclosure are less dangerous, normal siblings' forbidden thoughts, feelings, and fantasies emerge. To understand these nocturnal messages is to know what it really feels like to live with the Caliban Syndrome and where to begin to reverse its effects.

Damaged siblings figure prominently in the dreams of their normal brothers and sisters, often overtly. Although some of these dreams are populated by murderous maniacs and amorphous monsters that symbolize siblings who are frightening or overwhelming, most siblings appear recognizably as their daylight selves. Dreams specific to normal ones fall into three categories, all indicative of the unique, often unspoken burdens they shoulder, and some of which may overlap. Their predominant themes are the Magical Solution, the Awful Truth (my rape dream was of this type), and the Real Resolution (fortunately, my leaky office dream falls in this category).

the magical solution

The most common sibling theme in dreams is the intact sibling's desire to normalize the family by making the sibling's problem (or the problem sibling) go away. There are two ways to accomplish this—to repair damaged siblings by "arranging" for them to be magically healed, or to remove them by killing them off. Very rarely do normal siblings actually murder damaged relatives in cold blood in their dreams; more frequently they safely discharge their hidden hatred by "discovering" that the person has died.

Since dreamers are the authors and directors of their productions, they are responsible for everything that happens therein; nobody ever dies of natural causes in a dream. Rendering yourself the witness or the innocent bystander to fratricide is one way of disavowing the wish to commit it, while simultaneously expressing that very impulse. Susan Kim, the devoted caretaker of her retarded brother, reported occasional daydreams in which he died, always in an explosion of gore:

> Every once in a while I imagine something hideous happening to him—he's so vulnerable and totally trusting. I worry that he has high blood pressure, so his head blows up.

In reality she treats her brother with great gentleness, but she always feels she is not doing enough for him. All her violent thoughts find a safe outlet in her fantasy life or are directed against herself.

Amy Goodman, the young publicist who never went home so she could avoid seeing her schizophrenic brother wandering the streets, wants to have it both ways. Her dream expresses a longing to repair his destroyed life and another to rid her own of the havoc he wreaks:

> I can't remember if he became sicker and was institutionalized, or if he was curiously all better.

Most sibling dreamers opt for the unambivalent fantasy of the miraculous transformation that cures the sufferer, improves the siblings' relationship, and—because everything in a dream also reflects the dreamer—heals the self. Rebecca Ashford feels dreadful that she cannot tolerate any contact with her miserable, schizoid brother, so she fixes him up in her dreams:

He's completely normal. I walk in the room and say, "Danny, you look so good!"

"This is rare for me," she added sadly.

Physical and mental deformities alike disappear in dreams. Dancer Ashley King has two dysfunctional sisters—one borderline, the other bulimic—and is filled with shame and fear that she could turn into either one. "In my dreams," she says, "they are both really skinny and sane," so she can be too. Gloria Miller's relationship with a sister afflicted with Elephant Man's disease has been marred by mutual envy and hostility mixed with regret and sorrow. "I dream she's perfect and we have a wonderful time together," the healthy one says. In an unusual variation on the theme, Frank Gardiner makes his seriously retarded brother devious rather than damaged:

> I used to dream all the time that there was nothing wrong with him and that he was just faking.

Fixing the unfixable, or saving the irredeemable, is a frequent occurrence in sibling dreams. Marilyn Daniels, whose brother is serving a protracted sentence in the penitentiary for murdering a police officer, dreamed he saved her from rape; she made him prevent, rather than commit, a heinous crime. Marilyn converted her criminal brother into a hero, so she could look up to him rather than see him behind prison bars for the rest of their lives, at least while she slept.

Dreams in which a sibling no longer has the disability that prevents real contact or love between equals give a brief respite that is both painful and pleasing to recollect. Sarah Lattimer, whose sister

Mary is an ineducable, aggressive deaf-mute, had a recurring dream "like the Helen Keller movie. We had a wonderful afternoon together—I was her teacher, and we bonded." "To this day, I'm sensitive about Helen Keller jokes," she noted, wishing that her sister could resemble that extraordinary woman and that she herself could be "the miracle worker."

The fantasy of magical repair has multiple functions. It can be a dream come true, but it can also put a sibling on notice about the psychological work ahead. Jackie Hanson always longed for her mute, almost-twin sister to talk to her, although she knew it could never happen in waking life:

> Joan and I were assigned to separate groups. . . . Then all of a sudden she said one sentence: "I want to stay with you." I woke and remembered, "Oh my God, she spoke." It left me with a twinge of sadness.

Jackie understood that the dream announced the theme that would preoccupy her for years: creating her own autonomy by disentangling her identity from her sister's.

Normal ones often dream that a suffering sibling has died, or they discover to their astonishment that one who actually has died is still alive. In either version grief is strikingly absent. These dreams are an opportunity for "good" siblings to express death wishes too shocking or sinful to be stated outright; clergy and children of clergy are especially prone to them. A woman from a devout family, awaiting her fatally ill brother's demise with profoundly mixed emotions, dreamed:

I was home for Christmas, and he was there. We were sitting in the living room talking. All of a sudden I thought, "You're not supposed to be here, you're dead." Then I started to feel awful; I wanted somebody dead who's going to die.

A rabbi whose youth was marred by the inordinate attention his parents gave a quadriplegic brother who needed constant surgeries dreamed about the man's unwelcome resurrection:

Right after the funeral I dreamed that I saw him alive and well. I said, "Why are you here—aren't you supposed to be dead?"

The brother who had inadvertently robbed him of his childhood, a deprivation he had overtly borne without complaint, had not died for him psychologically, though he himself had officiated at the funeral. In the rabbi's unconscious his brother was still a lively presence who continued to affect him. Even posthumously Caliban will take up residence within you.

the awful truth

Dreams can remind normal siblings of the dark side of their relationship with an abnormal sibling. The purpose of these often terrifying nightmares is to prevent denial and call people's attention to anxiety-provoking information that it would be perilous to ignore.

Often the emotions rather than any specific content carry the message the dreamer needs to hear. Samantha Greenberg, who lived with amorphous fears about her retarded brother's potential for violence, regularly awoke in a cold sweat when he appeared in dreams that were too vague to pin down and too easy to discount. The only thing she recalled was "a feeling of panic that I don't know what he's going to do." Nobody in Samantha's family had considered him dangerous; her dream—especially because it recurred, as if to make her pay attention—warned her that it was true.

Unsavory facts about the sibling dreamer are highlighted in their dreams as well. Jane London felt too guilty and inhibited ever to raise her voice to the incompetent sister who was her lifelong burden; in the privacy of her own bedroom she said and did everything she publicly suppressed:

> I was shaking her and screaming at the top of my lungs. I felt bad afterward, but I've always been so frustrated and enraged with her.

Compassionate caretakers in waking life became furies in their dreams. Ellen O'Brian, the illustrator whose family expected her to attend far too much to her dull and demanding, severely learning-disabled sister, dreamed that her sister had a baby—a distinct possibility that Ellen dreaded in advance. "I was so angry that I was yelling at the whole family," she said, allowing herself to dream the reaction she would feel honor-bound to suppress when the blessed event actually occurred.

Images of witches are not confined to children's fairy tales or horror movies; they populate the dreams of normal siblings whose abnormal brothers and sisters are malevolent, frightening, or destructive. After her sister, who took good care of her when she was younger, turned vicious when she grew into an attractive rival, Jessica Kaplan repeatedly envisioned her as a witch. Candy Fine, the pregnant copywriter whose neurologically impaired brother threatened her security enough that she is leaving the country, found herself reliving scenes from the frightening film *The Blair Witch Project*, starring him:

> There's a feeling of supernatural doom, being in the woods. Babies and little children are in danger.

"Growing up, I always had the feeling that something weird would happen in my family, something irreparable," she said. She is taking drastic measures to protect her own future family.

Anxiety dreams are ubiquitous among pregnant women, but when a woman grows up with a sibling who has birth defects, the content is specific and literal. Candy also dreamed that "a friend is pregnant. The baby she's carrying is probably dead, but she would have to deliver it anyway."

This dream has layers of meanings beyond the universal ambivalence that maternity evokes. Candy is actually not sure whether her disturbed brother is psychically alive, and she wishes he were dead physically as well. The situation she dreams about also expresses her fear of contagion, deflected onto the ever-popular "friend" who stands in for herself; she is terrified that the child she carries could be emotionally dead like her brother and that she could do irreparable damage like her mother. She must "deliver" the dead baby to deal with her feelings about it; otherwise it will fester inside her and force her to run from the past forever.

Sometimes an anxiety dream expresses an internal as well as an external reality that is hard for the normal sibling to accept. Lisa Masterson, the "genetically engineered caretaker" of her drug-addicted brother and his progeny, washed her hands of the problem in a frequently repeated dream:

> My brother's in trouble, and I'm scared because I don't think I can help him.

Lisa is telling herself two truths—that reforming her brother is hopeless, and that she does not want to work at it anymore. She had the most recent rendition of this dream after spending a holiday weekend at the city jail trying, for what she swears is the last time, to get her brother released on bail.

real resolutions

Dreams that give a normal sibling clues to the way out of the Caliban Syndrome are not always enjoyable or easily comprehensible, but they are precious and memorable. They tend to occur when a normal one is struggling to understand the relationship with a damaged sibling. Such dreams are steadfast inner allies, offering advice, encouragement, and pointing out the path.

When advertising executive Barbara Green finally decided to begin psychotherapy after years of avoiding addressing the grievous multiple traumas of her childhood, her dreams cheered her on. In one she "went underwater and was still able to breathe." She was telling herself that if she goes into the depths of her unconscious, she will survive and neither drown nor be flooded with anxiety or sorrow. In another she "discovered a new experience"—confronting the past rather than running from it, as she did after her brother's suicide. In a third she told herself in symbolic terms about the task ahead of her:

> I'm a prisoner in a lovely suburban home—it's gorgeous, but if I step outside, I'm dead. My mother was guarding the door. I was trying to open a window, finding clever ways to escape.

Barbara is making efforts to "open a window," to let in the light and air of the present. She can indeed find a way to escape the deadly confinement of a life, like her mother's, that looked good on the surface—but she must first be clever enough to realize that she is imprisoning herself in it.

Carrie Grainger was puzzled that she was repeatedly "freaked out" by what she should have easily dismissed as just another "I'm back in school again" dream:

> I'm supposed to graduate from high school, but I've forgotten to show up in history class.

Carrie's beloved younger brother had a psychotic breakdown during her last year of high school. Her dream shows her that, like every normal sibling, she needs to study the past, to master the subject of her own history, before she can "graduate" from the Caliban Syndrome.

chapter 7

Invisibility and Perverse Preeminence

A TELEVISION ANCHORWOMAN RECOUNTED an image from her past that affected her profoundly, but that she knew would never be shown on the nightly news:

> My best friend in high school had a brother with cerebral palsy. I remember going to her house, and the first thing you saw when you walked in was a floor-to-ceiling blown-up photograph of him in his wheelchair—he'd been the CP poster child the year before he died. There wasn't a single picture of my friend, who had nothing wrong with her, anywhere in sight— and she was alive! It made me cry every time I went over there.

The reporter's friend was in an impossible position. How could she compete with a martyr, and how could she complain about favoritism when she alone was alive and well? Her friend shed the tears that she herself could only suppress with shame.

Invisible is the word normal children most often use to describe their place in the family, whether their damaged siblings are dead or alive. Their everyday trials and tribulations pale beside the catastrophe of their siblings' predicaments, so it seems natural that they should never come first; what is a parent to do when one child is throwing a fit of hysterics or having a seizure and the other wants help with her homework? The chronic overlooking is rarely intentional. Rather, it is what happens when desperate, overwhelmed adults with problems of their own try to cope with situations that no parent bargains for and few have the emotional resources to balance. As a result, many healthy siblings grow up with a hunger for attention that is never satisfied and that seems wrong to feel. Their needs, so consistently ignored, become invisible to themselves.

The alternative to being invisible is being all too visible, having a position of perverse preeminence in the family. Normal children who become the focus of their parents' dreams live anxiously in the spotlight and feel compelled to compensate for their damaged siblings; when you are "all I have left," as one father told his healthy daughter, everything depends on you. The obligation is crushing, and failing to live up to it is as devastating as having no right to attention; in fact, they are mirror images. Just as the invisible ones are expected to be mature and self-sufficient, the preeminent ones must excise their weaknesses, doubts, and contrary aspirations. In both cases part of the personality is lost.

To stay conscious of a normal child's requirements while coping with an abnormal one is a daunting task for even the most diligent of parents. The day my patient Peter Lehman's infant daughter was diagnosed with a severe spinal abnormality, he helplessly watched his healthy three-year-old son fade into the background as the retinue of neurologists, nurses, therapists, and anguished relatives descended upon the house. He felt himself being sucked into the maelstrom of caring for her and struggling to determine the proper treatment while trying to comfort his wife and handle his own anger, exhaustion, and depression. Because he had to detach from his feelings to conserve psychic energy, he knew that he could do little more than go through the motions with the boy. For years he was pursued by dreams that his son was in danger and that he was unable to rescue him. Fortunately his ability to empathize with his healthy child eventually limited the damage, but it cost years of anxiety and tension. A more typical and more pernicious scenario is for parents to manage stress and simplify their lives by eliminating awareness of the normal child's separate existence. If they think normal children need them less, they are not forced to make solomonic choices in allotting attention, or to be tormented by guilt about abandoning them, as Peter was.

There are several ways to make a normal child disappear: by focusing exclusively on the problem child, by permitting the problem child to violate the other child's rights, by assigning the normal one excessive responsibility, and by failing to acknowledge doing any of these things.

Ill children are squeaky wheels whom no parent should ignore, and tending them can indeed be all-consuming. The real problem, however, is not the time and effort spent but the parents' expectation that healthy children tolerate neglect for extensive periods without complaint—or agree that they are not being neglected at all.

"Everything was focused on the one who was sick," said Linda Simon, who lost track of how many operations her younger sister's intestinal abnormalities required. "I cried when she would go to the hospital because I wanted to go too—why couldn't I be ill?" She was so desperate to get her parents' attention that she took a drug overdose as a teenager. "It was my way of saying, 'I'm here too, don't forget me.' The family went into counseling as a result." Linda eventually found a constructive way to realize her childhood wish: she became a nurse. Attention given and received is clearly still a matter of great concern for her, since she went out of her way to assure me that if I called at a particular time for our interview, I would be guaranteed her "undivided attention."

These children go to various lengths to get noticed, from dying their hair purple to trying to kill themselves. One woman remembered announcing to her mother at age three that she wanted to be a butterfly; that way she would be recognized for her beauty, and she could also escape. But few are able to overcome their parents' powerful need to ignore them.

Normality is a liability in some families. A deformity (and its meaning to a parent) can be the reason to prefer a damaged child, or it can legitimize a preference actually based on other factors. Cindy Goodman's mother made her feel that she never measured up to her brother, whom she favored because he was a boy. His cleft palate—for which his classmates labeled him "Mushmouth"—was a way to rationalize the inordinate attention she paid him, an additional reason he was special. "He had the obvious problem, yet I felt I had one," this retired guidance counselor said. "My mother constantly asked me, 'Why can't you be more like him?' and I always felt handicapped by being normal, as well as female. He was picked on as a child, so she had a sense of pity and compassion for him that she didn't have for me. He got all kinds of special attention—she gave him a present every time he had an operation. I didn't understand it, but I remember accepting that I'd never deserve as much. He grew up to be extremely successful, the best and the brightest. When I finally graduated from college at the age of thirty, my shining hour, my mother called to ask if she could give me the same present that she had gotten him for his last birthday."

Cindy's mother, like many parents, was entirely unaware of her behavior and its impact on her daughter. "I told my mother recently what she had done, and she had no idea. She insisted that she had treated us exactly alike," Cindy said. Her childhood experience had one positive effect; it made Cindy sensitive to justice and inclusion in her professional as well as her personal life.

Parents are often tempted to make compensatory gestures to problem children or to treat them with a spurious equality that diminishes the uniqueness of the normal one. They buy the unmarriageable sister the same dishes and linens as the bride, and they reflexively offer the crippled brother "the best seat in the house." But even forever sharing or ceding the limelight is not as damaging as forfeiting the right to object.

Patterns of preference can outlast the disability. Marcey Gibson's elder sister wore a brace to correct scoliosis when she was a child, which made her the object of their mother's solicitude. Thirty years later the mother still calls Marcey by her sister's name.

Gloria Miller's sister, deformed by Elephant Man's disease, was labeled "Duck-Ass" by her classmates. To spare the girl further torment, Gloria's mother forbade Gloria to invite friends to the house; hypersensitivity to one child's feelings made her insensitive to the other's. Gloria had a recurrent dream common among healthy siblings: that she had a room of her own—an inviolate space that was hers alone. The symbols normal children use to depict their siblings can be even more explicit and less benign; in her dreams financial adviser Maggie Payne's uncontrollable sister, who never forgave her for refusing to ask her to be her maid of honor ("I wanted my wedding to be the one thing in my life she didn't spoil," said Maggie), became an amorphous monster crawling up the sidewalk and taking up all the room on the street where their family lived.

The automatic sympathy that parents extend to problem children in an effort to mitigate their pain often becomes a license for those children to misbehave. When Ben Ramsey's brother, jealous of his academic success, stabbed him in a fight, their parents exhorted them both not to "play so rough." "He had carte blanche in the family," said Ben. "Because they couldn't get angry at him, they got angry at me."

Siblings of the handicapped are given far more onerous responsibilities than other children. The issue is not the tasks themselves but being taken for granted. Since she was a little girl, nineteen-year-old Jamie Walters has been diapering her microcephalic elder sister and curtailing her own after-school activities to stay with her. "I never minded taking care of her," she said. "I resented that my mother didn't acknowledge that I was helping." They long for the very recognition and appreciation of their sacrifices that, paradoxically, their parents are incapable of providing.

Some children have to be mute as well as invisible—neither seen nor heard. Hospital administrator Jennifer Martin was designated the bearer of the unspeakable truth about her brother's fate, and it almost destroyed her. Throughout her childhood she saw him became progressively incapacitated by muscular dystrophy ("I stared raw powerlessness in the face") and had to uncomplainingly accept when his frustration turned to violence directed against her. Then, as a seventh-grader, reading about the illness for a science project, she discovered to her horror that his condition was fatal— a fact that her parents had concealed from her. Unable to contain this awful information alone, she confided in a school counselor, who mentioned it without her permission in a family therapy session. "My parents felt that I had betrayed them. They wept and said they didn't know how he would live through knowing it—I'm feeling suicidal from guilt, and this is what they're worried about. I felt bound and gagged by the situation." Jennifer looked fruitlessly for books to help her cope with the combination of grief, rage, self-hatred, and helplessness she felt as a sibling of a seriously ill brother, and she finally found some insights in the literature on families of alcoholics. "I share the disability of our family," she concluded. "Our family *was* a disability. Not only did they treat me as not important, but I treat myself this way. Therapy has helped me honor myself even if they could not."

TO BE CHOSEN is more insidious than to be invisible, as I know from my own experience; specialness, though overtly preferable, extracts its own price. "I had to be perfect," said a woman whose life goal was to make up to her parents for her brother's fecklessness. "They put all their hopes on me. It didn't matter who I was; I had to be more. I carried the weight of having to be normal and functioning and achieving—I never had the right to be immature in any way, to act out or stamp my foot. I was the Rock of Gibraltar. Even if you're successful, you never really feel lucky." Preeminence, which requires children to mold their personalities to their parents' specifications, is perverse because it distorts the self.

Children with damaged siblings who are designated the bearers of their parents' destinies experience more pressure than other children because the demands placed on them are double—they must simultaneously fulfill parental aspirations and compensate for their sibling's failure to do so. Everything depends on them. Living with the concrete example of what not to be intensifies the chosen one's anxiety and urgency to succeed at this impossible task. Their compulsion to achieve is a crushing symptom of the Caliban Syndrome.

The fallout from being invisible is to become self-effacing; perverse preeminence breeds perfectionism, morbid self-criticism, and fear of failure. Internalizing parents' exacting standards, chosen children become compulsive compensators who cannot tolerate any aspect of themselves reminiscent of their siblings. For them, excelling is not an ideal; it is an emotional life preserver.

The perfections they are required to attain can take the form of actions, achievements, or feelings; a normal child in the spotlight must be unfailingly good, successful, or happy in order not to forfeit the precarious position as the one who is favored and who does not disappoint.

For Christine White, a minister's daughter with hyperactive twin brothers, not only her parents but the entire congregation dictated how she should act: "Our family had to be a shining example of godliness and perfect behavior—and I had to double my perfect behavior so the parishioners wouldn't think less of my parents because they couldn't control my brothers."

Compensating for a sibling by succeeding academically is usually a conscious project and tends to become an obsession early on. A young chemist, frantic with tension about falling down on the job, recalled that even in grade school she was "the only child who used to cry over workbook exercises." She bore this responsibility in silence; "I never was willing or able to ask for any help because I didn't want them to know I had any problems."

As teenagers, such children inhibit their natural rambunctiousness and rebelliousness. "I never let myself be reckless," said the sister of a boy who was always in trouble. "In high school I never stayed out late or got drunk. I made sure to spend weekends at home and never violated a curfew because I didn't want my parents to worry." Having to be exemplary constricts their self-expression and makes them wistful for the wildness other children consider their birthright.

Katie Clark, a web page designer, was acutely aware that she had to achieve for three. "My older autistic brother had a difficult time finding and keeping a job even with help, and my younger depressed sister had even more of a struggle. My parents couldn't expect as much from them as they do from me, so I felt immense pressure to succeed because the others wouldn't. I had to be the normal one—the high achiever who got good grades and became well established in my career. I've never been able to drop the shackles of responsibility for a moment." To be what she defined as irresponsible—traveling cross-country instead of working without a break—would seem perilously close to her siblings in her own as well as in her parents' eyes.

Like invisible children, preeminent ones keep their struggles out of sight, though one young man was so crushed by expectations that he dared to confess to his father. "He wanted me to be a doctor, but I finally told him, 'I'm just average, and it's not going to get any better.' I just want to be like everybody else and not have to try so hard all the time." To relax and be himself is to fail.

For Jackie Hanson, who was eight years old when her autistic sister ate her book report cover, the demands were emotional. "My perfection was in my feelings," she said. "I spent my childhood making up for my sister who couldn't function. I would not let on that I was upset. I was always tuned in to what others were feeling and not tuned in to myself, so I became the agreeable, quiet kid. I was so restrained because she was so much the opposite." Vigilance to her parents' needs required her to suppress her own personality and force herself into the mold of "not my sister" that she later spent years trying to break.

The role that one woman (who later became a comedienne) called the "little sunbeam" is especially popular in damaged families. To have at least one child who is cheerful—and therefore not hopeless, furious, or tyrannical—eases demoralized parents; to be that special child is to have the power to make your parents smile, no matter what the cost in self-estrangement.

Bringing his parents joy has always been Jeff Myer's job. The mission assigned to him, and that he embraced, was to be the anodyne for the anguish caused by his suicidally depressed older brother. His naturally buoyant and resilient disposition suited him for the task of dispelling the pall that his brother's moodiness, antagonism, and despair cast over the family. "He never had friends, and you had to walk on eggshells around him," Jeff said, "so my job was to neutralize that. My parents coddled me in some ways and set impossible goals in others. I was expected to approach life with ease—to be carefree, easygoing, light rather than heavy, sociable rather than sullen. I had an explanation ready for everything that could be perceived as a problem, and they were eager to buy it; they couldn't bear another child crippled by unhappiness."

Having to be happy all the time because a sibling is always wretched is hard work. To accomplish this feat, Jeff trained himself early on to eliminate any untoward reaction automatically. Without being fully aware of his motives, he ceaselessly cultivated good moods because he risked turning into his brother if he ever lapsed into a bad one; with practice he became so adept that dark thoughts barely registered. This skill had the paradoxical effect of causing him to feel disconnected from all his emotions and intensely anxious lest a negative one slip past his early warning system. Enforced, artificial positive thinking made him intensely miserable.

Jeff was unable to remove the smiley face when he left home; the obligation to be happy had become a habit. As an adult, he constantly monitors his contentment quotient, lest he fall short of his own lofty standard; despite his considerable achievements, everyone else seems more successful and more satisfied than he.

The breakup of his marriage when he turned thirty-five put Jeff into a tailspin that even his best efforts could not completely reverse; here was a failure that partook of his brother's. When, for the first time in his life, he told his mother how upset he was, she said only partly in jest, "You were supposed to be my happy child." Her statement showed him the source of his self-imposed vocation; he understood how much the need to be cheerful had originally been external and had cut him off from experiencing or processing even normal grief. "My life as I've constructed it has always been fragile, and my ability to love or even know myself has been precarious," he said, almost welcoming the authentic painful emotion.

What happens when, after spending your childhood molding your personality to fit others' specifications, you grow up and suddenly have nobody to please but yourself? Illustrator Ellen O'Brian faced this common predicament of the preeminent child when she felt at a complete loss on her first unsupervised job: "I'm the only functioning sibling of three in my family, so I got a heavy dose of 'you can do anything.' My parents pushed me ahead in school. I thought, 'I'll be the best artist'—it was important to do really well, and I did. Then I had to prove myself to my teachers—even though I was aware of it, I couldn't stop it. I thought I was perfect."

As long as she had some authority figure in loco parentis, Ellen could recapitulate the role of the high-achieving special child that had been her lifeline. But entering the world of independent professional work required different skills: "I do well when I get feedback, when someone's noticing, but it's hard to carry things out on my own." With nobody to praise her and none of the obvious yardsticks of success by which she had formerly measured her achievement now available, she "floundered around." There were days, she discovered to her distress, when she found it impossible to motivate herself, when she felt uninterested in her work, and when she resented having to cater to her clients' whims. These normal reactions, so foreign to her and so threatening to her persona, paralyzed her with insecurity and self-doubt. "All my life I had responsibilities I didn't want," she told me, "even if they were just emotional—I had to do well to support my parents and make them feel good. This career is the first thing I've pursued just for myself, and I feel like a wreck. Part of me runs away from that responsibility and can't take the freedom. I feel really shaky now that nobody is seeing or hearing about my work, and I'm having trouble gauging if I'm on the right track." Ellen recognizes that with no higher authority to conform to, she must finally learn to answer to herself.

INVISIBILITY AND PERVERSE PREEMINENCE are obverses, complementary yet intersecting roles thrust upon the normal sibling by traumatized and unconscious parents. Both are types of abandonment; the requirements of the invisible and of the preeminent are lost in the shadow of their "special needs" siblings—a euphemism that excuses ignoring them or making impossible demands on them. This concept, which has gained wide acceptance in the contemporary world, is in fact a form of affirmative action in the family that has the unintended effect of denigrating the concept of normality. It is a covert form of discrimination against normal children; the sibling of the child with special needs is not supposed to have any needs.

Jackie Hanson, who experienced firsthand the damage this mentality wreaked in her own family and grew up to become a professional advocate for the disabled, believes that no child is well served by defining abnormality away:

> I don't make apologies for using the word *normal*. To be afraid to say that someone like my sister is not normal is denying reality—normal is defined in the dictionary as "like the majority." I don't use the term *child with special needs* either

because normal children like me have special needs too—ours are very special, unique, and neglected. This way of thinking does a disservice to the nondisabled and connotes that their needs don't count. Society needs to deny the consequences of differences, and it sugarcoats them for parents. This doesn't really help at all, but most don't go down the insight road.

The "special needs" mentality automatically enlists normal children in a crusade on behalf of damaged siblings. The loneliness, anxiety, perfectionism, and loss of emotional freedom that result from being forced into either of these impossible positions are exacerbated by the corollary assumption that normal children should be relieved and grateful not to have special needs. They are thereby denied what ought to be a universal birthright—to be recognized, appreciated, and nurtured as unique individuals, whether handicapped or healthy.

chapter 8

Dark Victories

IT IS A SCENE OUT OF A NORMAN ROCKWELL illustration. A teenage girl sits at her dressing table putting the final touches on her hair and makeup for the prom. Nervous but excited, she gazes at herself in the mirror. Behind her, watching the preparations with rapt attention, sits her little sister. Someday, we know and they know, her turn will come.

But a damaged sibling's turn never comes. The sister who watches so wistfully may even be older. She will spend that evening, and most subsequent evenings, in front of the television. Eventually you will move out and create an independent life full of possibilities she cannot imagine. She may (perhaps at your mother's insistence) be a bridesmaid, but never a bride. She may not go to college. While you mature, pursue a career, and find a husband, she will stay home, or have a marginal existence with a menial job, or spend years in an institution or in and out of the hospital. How can you deserve your bounty when she is doomed?

Under normal circumstances sibling rivalry is an inevitable, if highly charged, part of growing up. Competition between equals, as ferocious and wounding as it can be, rarely provokes paralyzing guilt because the victory is not a unilateral, uncontested triumph over an adversary whose defeat is a foregone conclusion. But the success of a normal child is forever tarnished by seeming to come at the abnormal child's expense; natural joy at winning feels unseemly, even immoral. Rivalry distorted by disability cannot simply fade, evolve, or be accepted; the implicit contrast with the sibling's fate always lurks accusingly in the shadows.

Intact children find their siblings' envy of their social and professional success and their physical health as disturbing as their own pleasure in beating the competition so decisively. Fear that they have no right to their ill-gotten gains drives them to conceal or sabotage their achievements or to spend their lives attempting to compensate their "victims." Even when they suffer no apparent remorse, as I never did, a nameless anxiety haunts them and makes everything they have seems tenuous or undeserved. Survivor guilt is a major component of the Caliban Syndrome.

JANE LONDON'S STRANGE, partially blind, and inept younger sister was her "assistant" when she got ready for dates in high school. "I used to feel bad about her watching me, but it didn't stop me because kids are also into themselves," she recalled. "In school I was outgoing and a high achiever—she always quit everything. After she didn't get into the sorority I was in, I tried to help her find activities she'd like. Then she quit college and tried to throw herself down the stairs." Jane was so troubled by her sister's defeats—and the implicit comparison to her own social and academic success—that she visited her sister's psychiatrist to ask if she could do anything to help. Guilt prevented her from following his excellent advice: "Let her come to you."

While her sister continued to live at home and work sporadically as a Kmart cashier, Jane, by then a happily married guidance counselor, became pregnant with her first child. Dreading the impact of her twin triumphs, Jane was seized with a compulsive need to mend her sister's unremediable plight; only by filling the void in her sister's life could she deserve to enjoy the fullness of her own. She had a dream that combined her worst conscious—and entirely realistic—fear with her most unconscious, unacceptable wish:

> I dreamed that my sister was never going to get married and that she'd commit suicide. This put me into a huge depression. It was like a strong premonition, almost a prophecy, so I tried to fix her up with every single male I knew, in a frantic effort to get her to connect. I thought I had to rescue her; it was up to me to save her from her fate. I felt despair about her empty life but never told anybody about it—I just carried it around because I thought nobody would understand, and I was also afraid that if I talked too much about her, people would think maybe I was crazy too.

In addition to their unrealistic expectations that they can alter their sibling's destinies, normal siblings are prey to malignant grandiosity, the fantasy that they have the power to destroy their rivals by succeeding. They irrationally believe that they can cause or exacerbate a sibling's failure. Both convictions are based on the fallacy that

their fates and their siblings' are interlocked. Jane thought that seeing the glaring discrepancy between them would kill her sister; not
being able to save her meant forfeiting her own right to happiness,
and becoming depressed like her was her punishment. She had to
keep her despair secret to shore up the crumbling boundary
between them in her own mind.

The nightmare came true only partially. Jane's sister never did
marry, but she is still eking out a life thirty years later. Jane is still
trying to find ways to compensate—paying her insurance, taking
her on trips—that never fully eradicate the guilt.

There is a critical difference between assisting a damaged sibling and trying to undo accidents of fate and fortune that you cannot help and did not cause. The former is brotherly or sisterly love
and mature, if circumscribed, responsibility. The latter is compulsive self-sacrifice driven by the belief that you do not deserve your
advantages. The one is sadly finite; the other never lets you go.

Jane's childhood attempt to "find activities" for her dysfunctional sister is a common undertaking, born of compassion, the
desire for companionship, and the need to salve a troubled conscience. Ellen O'Brian, the illustrator who struggled to become self-
directed as an adult, also remembers trying "to engage and entertain"
her learning-disabled sister by "creating games we could play
together" even as a little girl. Men in particular report having to rein
in their physical competitiveness with their less able brothers, often
at their parents' urging. Paul Morrison, a thirty-five-year-old systems analyst whose older brother is neurologically impaired, said
with a nervous laugh, "Boys wrestle, and so did we, until I realized I
shouldn't do it because he couldn't fight back—I would have
whipped him too badly." Since young children make no distinctions

between thoughts and actions, he believed that his desire to beat his brother literally as well as symbolically could be deadly and must be suppressed. Viewing all natural competitiveness as destructive leads to an unrealistic sense of responsibility for a sibling's life.

It is human nature to want to be the star, but nobody who is related to a friendless outcast enjoys her popularity unambivalently. Carolyn Johnson's older brother is a "high-functioning autistic—intelligent but geeky, with no concept of politeness. I sense how jealous he is that I have a social life, and he doesn't know how to go about having one himself. I feel awful when he asks me 'How do you make friends?' because I know I can't tell him things he can use." She may be a social success, but as an adviser to her lonely brother, she is worthless.

At significant moments—making the honor roll when your brother is brain-damaged, dancing in a recital when your sister is paralyzed—it is excruciating to know how much better off you are and always will be. Paul's friend helped him temporarily finesse such a moment on his wedding day:

> Right before the ceremony my brother got emotional. He said, "I'm older, I should be getting married before you." My best man calmed him down by saying his younger brother got married first too.

It took some prodding to get Paul to admit that the situations were not really comparable and that his best man's reassurance provided a comforting pretense that only smoothed over a yawning gap in their fortunes, providing fleeting solace for them both. Failing to acknowledge that his own life is so much better through no virtue of his own has trapped Paul in a cycle of appeasing his brother and then resenting the imposition, of which his behavior at the wedding was only a symptom.

To offer their less fortunate siblings at least a momentary experience of prevailing, normal siblings try to level the playing field. Paul used to throw board games to let his brother win. Manny Resnick went much farther; he threw away a brilliant career for the sake of his obsessive-compulsive brother Marc.

Marc's disadvantages weighed heavily on Manny, who had always been their physician father's favorite. "His purity mania, belching, and odd/even compulsions made life miserable," Manny said. "He feels my father never respected him, that I got all the positive vibes and he got the negative. There's some truth to that, because he does things that upset everybody, but it still made me feel bad—the only thing you can think is that you're responsible." Manny's victory over Marc for their father's affections—a competition every sibling wants to win—was too crushing for him to enjoy; he is spending his life trying to expiate retroactively by making this victory pyrrhic.

The fear of contagion that intact siblings battle caused Manny to "shut Marc out" in adolescence, a time when self-definition is particularly tenuous. Although Manny knew he "had the same tendencies" toward the disorder, he felt both guilty and relieved that he was not incapacitated by it. To further safeguard his sanity, Manny "cut the tether" binding the brothers together when he left for college and rarely called or visited Marc. "I felt terrible but happy to get out," Manny admitted, "but he fell apart when I left. I was struggling for emotional equilibrium, and he pulled me down—it was the only way I could survive."

What could have been a natural parting of the ways in another family became charged and ominous because one brother lost his way. Manny failed to realize that Marc would have floundered whether he had been there or not.

Manny was right, however, that severing the fraternal tie freed him. He had a stellar undergraduate academic career and got accepted to the top two medical schools in the country, while Marc flunked out of college and told nobody but him. With Manny's encouragement, Marc found psychiatric help, finished school—and decided that he too wanted to become a physician.

The elder brother faced a terrible choice: "Medical school was my brother's bid for my father's approval. I didn't want to take away his only chance, the last thing that was his own, so I withdrew my applications at the last minute. I didn't go, so as not to compete with him; my goal was clearing space for my brother to be okay." To do otherwise would have been to seek the favoritism he had always passively enjoyed. Often, as in Manny's case, the guilt the higher-functioning person feels is deflected from pleasure at his own advantages to distress at the other's hardships. Manny had to sacrifice his ambitions to save not only his brother but his image of himself as a brother.

But clearing space so radically was not punishment enough for a lifetime of prevailing; in graduate school Manny unwittingly took on his brother's depression and the full brunt of his symptoms: "It finally got to me. I had the same problems he had had as an undergraduate but that were unusual for me—writer's block, hopelessness, the same repetitive thoughts—I hit a wall. I felt stupid and angry for painting myself into a corner." He understood his problems not as self-inflicted punishment and identification with Marc but as evidence that he was doomed to share his brother's fate.

Like Jane's nightmare, Manny's fears came true only partially, and his solution worked only partially. Manny recovered psychologically, married, and made a name for himself as director of a major cultural organization, a profession that suited him better than medicine because it was independent of obligations. ("I was headed toward psychiatry, with some unconscious idea that I was going to cure my family, so in that sense it was freeing not to become a doctor.") Mark did attend medical school, but his life has continued to be problematic even with the M.D.; "he ended up crusting over his earlier wounds—he manages to keep going professionally, but his private life's a mess."

Highly successful siblings like Manny are especially prone to feelings of omnipotence; as people of action, they cannot bear to know that they can do nothing to erase the discrepancies between them and their siblings. Despite the enormity of his sacrifice, Manny still does not believe that he has done enough for Marc: "I'm not a good brother, I'm a failure as an older brother. I still distance myself from him; I don't call him as much as I should. I'm not the friend and counselor I should be to him. I'm still afraid—afraid of social embarrassment—and on a deeper level I worry I still could be dragged down into depression and mental illness like him." Assuming that Marc would appreciate being "counseled" is a form of subtle condescension. Manny's obsessive fears that he mistreats his brother by separating from him and that he resembles Marc more than he does are the only ways their lives are actually alike. Marc is obsessed with everything; Manny is still obsessed with Marc. Manny clings to the notion that his intercession could improve Marc's life; guilt is often preferable to helplessness.

A brother who steps aside to promote a sibling professionally can consider himself a good samaritan even if his efforts yield mixed results, but a brother who steps into the only arena where his problem sibling excels feels like a usurper and a spoiler. Normal children assume they must automatically defer and squelch any striving that may detract from the other's constricted sphere of competence; to aspire is to supplant, and to compete is to steal. The implied comparison to their sibling's lesser achievements is a whispered accusation, never far from consciousness.

The one unassailable talent that Ben Ramsey's older brother David possessed was his beautiful singing voice. David, who had attacked Ben with a knife when they were children, had "lots of different start-and-stop careers" and even managed to get himself thrown out of the Peace Corps in his twenties. Aside from occasional gigs with bands and solo performances with church choirs, David, now sixty years old, has been supported by his parents, while Ben—a fine amateur singer himself—worked his way up to a job as a buyer in a department store. The brothers had finally reached an uneasy truce, when a thrilling and unexpected invitation came Ben's way at age forty-five. "A friend's daughter was getting married and asked me to sing at her wedding. I was excited and honored but very worried about performing, since David is a professional musician," said Ben. The night before his debut, he had a liberating nightmare:

> I dreamed I was wandering through a maze and couldn't find the wedding. I was tremendously anxious that I was going to be late. When I finally got there, David was already sitting at the back of the stage. Then I forgot what I was supposed to sing. He began to cue me, but when I tried to do it, I totally

choked. I had no voice—I couldn't squeeze out the first note. I woke up horrified that I wasn't going to be able to do it.

Fortunately, Ben's fears were groundless: "When I stood up and sang in reality, all my fears vanished—this dream was a real turning point. It revealed my inhibition to supplant my brother, so it is interesting that he did not steal the show. That was a big deal." Ben must have felt punished enough for his ambition by the dream (and relieved that his dream-brother gave him permission by assisting) to feel entitled to find his voice. Having a brother's blessing—even if it is self-generated—legitimizes competitive feelings that might otherwise seem far too dangerous to act on.

What happens if a brother is so disabled that he will never have any area of expertise and feels nothing but impotent envy and anguish at his sister's superior abilities? Twenty-seven-year-old Sandy Wilson tries to manage her brain-damaged older brother Michael's jealousy and her own guilt by preempting even the possibility of achievement. "If I succeed, it takes away from what he has," Sandy reasons, so this hardworking and talented young woman subtly thwarts herself at every turn. That Michael suffered his injuries at birth and still shows vestiges of the intellect that would have been his exacerbates her extreme self-effacement. "I haven't been able to commit to anything or anybody because I know he would resent me even more bitterly than he does already," she says, as though she could regulate her brother's emotional state by lying low.

Sandy struggles to meet two contradictory and equally urgent demands: compensating her parents for their disappointment in her brother by being a perfect, self-sufficient and successful daughter, driven by the compulsion to achieve, and simultaneously protecting her brother from knowing about these accomplishments. Her own desire for self-expression gets buried somewhere in between. She tries to compromise by never letting herself do anything—at least overtly—that Michael cannot; ambition and compassion battle within her.

Sandy has found some ingenious ways around her dilemma: "I chose a women's college because he couldn't have gone there even if he could have attended college, so it was my own space." The campus had the additional advantage of being thousands of miles away, so she could conceal her achievements more successfully. After failing her driving test twice at home because she "felt so bad that he could never drive," she allowed herself to pass on the third try by taking the test far from Michael.

Geographic solutions like Sandy's are common; having the sibling out of sight puts him at least temporarily out of mind, and the person can feel freer to find herself without having to witness his resentment. Of course, since the sibling's image is still carried within, real and lasting separation occurs only when the control that the image exerts diminishes.

Sibling-related guilt is so compelling that normal children tend to attribute more of their conflicts to it than is actually the case and ignore other issues in their lives. Much of Sandy's anxiety is self-generated, so that even though she is now living in her "own space," she continues to restrict herself emotionally and intellectually for reasons that have little to do with Michael. She has yet to select a career and avoids getting seriously involved with any man—"I'm afraid to date because he can't," she explains; her brother's distress, while real, is also a convenient excuse. Like many healthy siblings, she is so obsessed with dealing with her afflicted brother that she has not paid sufficient attention to problems that are only superficially related to him; many young women with successful brothers—or no brothers—have paralyzing fears of intimacy and trouble defining their professional identities. The problems with Michael are serious and real, but they are not the only problems Sandy faces.

Sandy's anxiety increases as her desires for a relationship and for creative outlets get stronger and harder to resist. If she is to fulfill herself, she must accept a painful but ultimately comforting fact that every normal sibling must face: even if she accomplishes nothing, she has already surpassed her brother because she has a fully functioning brain and he never will—the "damage" is done. One manifestation of grandiosity is to imagine that you are more central to a brother's self-esteem than you really are; another is to believe that you would be problem-free without him. Sandy's brother probably has a greater influence on her feelings than she has on his. Since he will feel bereft and envious whatever she does—and probably not as much as she projects onto him—in the words of Dorothy Parker, she might as well live.

Internalized guilt about success can last a lifetime, long after a sibling could be directly affected. Once a sense of nonentitlement becomes part of a person's identity and set of assumptions about the world, it is extraordinarily hard to shake. Fifty years after Maggie Payne's embittered, enraged sister stopped talking to her for refusing to make her maid of honor, Maggie still hides her light under a barrel. As if to protect herself retroactively from her sister's envy, Maggie never feels pride in anything she accomplishes. "I made a killing in the stock market, but I couldn't enjoy it or even acknowledge it," Maggie confessed, as if her "killing" had actually killed someone. "I didn't tell anybody. It's as if nothing of mine has any importance. I need to see myself as a person who doesn't have anything, and if I do achieve something, it's got nothing to do with me—all the good things about my kids I attribute to them. My mother told me I was responsible for my sister's misery and I believed her, but I think I would have felt it anyway—my sister was paranoid, friendless, and depressed and extraordinarily envious of everything I did."

Not only what siblings say but what parents convey makes people like Maggie feel undeserving of a good life. They must watch their self-defeating attitude and work constantly to counteract the deep-rooted convictions that interfere with their appreciation of what they create, in difficult circumstances.

Many healthy siblings imagine that they can help a sibling succeed or at least prevent a failure by holding themselves back, but this is clearly impossible when the person has committed a terrible crime. Law-abiding brothers and sisters can feel compelled to self-destruct, as if to repent for crimes they should have been able to prevent. Kinship makes them involuntary participants.

Marilyn Daniels was the only stable influence on her younger brother Sam; their parents were violent alcoholics who virtually abandoned both children. Marilyn, like Manny, was lucky in her personality and labored to make the best of her natural advantages; "I always had an easier time in life than he did—I don't know why," she said. She remembers constantly getting Sam, an intelligent but wretchedly lonely, hyperactive child, out of scrapes that became more frightening as he got older: "I always had him in tow, and he was angry all the time." The only member of her extended family who was not a felon, she was the stable, hardworking, reliable one; he was a drug addict by the time he was fourteen. When she could no longer cope with Sam's escalating violence and criminality, Marilyn left town and worked her way through college. She had had only minimal contact with her wayward brother for several years when she heard a chilling report on the radio:

> The announcer said a policeman had been killed in a drug bust downtown, by a guy carrying a .38. For some reason I knew it was Sam—he was twenty-three at the time. I took all my clothes off, took two showers, dressed again, and drove around aimlessly for hours.

Just as Manny preferred to feel guilty over his brother's woes rather than accept his inability to reverse them, Marilyn's actual inability to prevent the murder was less tolerable to her than a fantasized culpability for it. She felt her destiny was linked to Sam's, that somehow she shared responsibility for his crime—and that she too had to pay:

> Part of my DNA did that. I felt I was implicated—even though I understand I couldn't have stopped him, I still feel somehow I should have—if only I'd stuck around a little bit longer.

Marilyn had been on her way to class when she heard the news, but she never made it back. "I skipped out of my finals—I tried not to drop out of school, but I couldn't. I drank and smoked for two years." She could not bear to succeed when her brother had failed so disastrously. As if to prove their resemblance, she punished herself by unleashing on herself a less lethal form of the destructiveness he had turned on another. She not only hid her light, as Maggie did; she almost extinguished it. The more disastrous the failure, the more extreme is a sibling's reaction.

For the first three years of his fifty-five-years-to-life sentence, Marilyn sentenced herself to rehabilitate Sam. To atone for the "crime" of abandoning him, she sent Sam money and books about "religion, psychology, and success" and went into debt to pay his appeal lawyer's retainer; "I still believed I could be his savior," she said. Then she had a dream that granted her permission to take care of herself once again:

> I dreamed that he decided to change careers, that he'd get another job in jail—that there would be some change, that he'd actually have some choices. It made me cry. Afterward I started to allow myself to do things.

Prior to this dream, Marilyn had seen her brother as the prisoner of his fate; now she understood that he had choices, even in jail. Because she believed that their fates were linked, this was her way to relieve herself from annihilating guilt; she could return to college and feel she had a right to prosper. Even profoundly damaged siblings are responsible for their actions and can exercise their wills; recognizing this reality gives their relatives permission to exercise their own wills.

To finally have your home, your parents, or your life to yourself when a sibling is institutionalized or dies is another dreadful victory—one that almost cost Jennifer Martin her life. Jennifer, who had accidentally discovered that her violent but talented brother's degenerative disease would eventually kill him, once screamed at him, "I wish you would hurry up and die," when he beat her and seriously considered suicide afterward. "I must be a monster for hating him," she remembers feeling. "How could I want him to die when he was going to die? Therapy helped me realize that anybody in my position feels like that, and I just voiced it." Jennifer and her brother were partially reconciled by the time he died, after great suffering. "His death was a relief to the whole family, even though they were shocked when I admitted it out loud," she said, finally accepting the excruciating mixture of relief, pity, and guilt that anyone would feel, without hating either her brother or herself.

As trying as it was to live with the sister who ate her homework, it was devastating to lose her. Jackie Hanson recalled the awful moment when her mute, hyperactive almost-twin left for the group home where Jackie knew she would spend the rest of her life. "I had promised her she would never have to go," Jackie said, "and here I was going back on my word, although it couldn't be helped and she ended up much happier there." A woman whose retarded brother blasted the radio at dawn daily wept when she saw the expression on his face as he signed the papers that would send him away for good, even though she greedily anticipated the quiet. However much havoc a deeply damaged sibling wreaks, it is hard not to believe that the freedom and comfort you enjoy when he departs are bought by an innocent person's imprisonment.

Normal siblings face a formidable task from which others are exempt: to succeed when their closest relative fails. They must embrace the fortunate yet tragic accident that no action of theirs can alter: that they were born with the undeserved advantage of a sounder mind or body—that they are the normal ones, fated to live a normal life. Simply being whole is the darkest victory of all.

They need to learn that, despite their competitive urges, they have not intentionally built their good fortune on the ruins of another's. They have to understand that self-expression and fulfillment are inalienable rights that having a dysfunctional sibling does not require them to forfeit. Feeling this freedom involves learning to tolerate guilt, accept limitations, and recognize that their victories, however dark, defeat no one. They are hard-won, legitimate achievements worth celebrating.

chapter 9

Passing Caliban On: Normal Siblings as Parents

PEOPLE ALWAYS TRY to make different mistakes than their parents, and they always fail. As parents, normal children are especially prone to repeating sibling experiences; their reactions to their own children combine how their parents behaved and how they felt as siblings themselves. Like all parents, normal siblings pick particular offspring to be new editions of their own brothers and sisters—the more troubled the tie to the originals, the more involuntary and arbitrary the projection. Despite their best efforts, they perpetuate past family patterns in unexpected ways; the actors change, but the script remains the same.

Anxiety that their new family will recapitulate their old one can be quite conscious; one woman said, "My brother represents all the fears I would have if I had children." It is no accident that a disproportionate number of normal siblings choose not to reproduce.

Although your children do not have to be disabled to evoke painful feelings about damaged siblings, having a troubled child of your own after you grew up with one feels like déjà vu all over again. It is impossible to avoid reliving the original emotions—especially the ones you carefully erased the first time around.

Barbara Green fled the scene after her beloved brother, only one year her senior, committed suicide at twenty-two. She doesn't even remember the date he asphyxiated himself in the very car in which he had taught her to drive. "I never asked about the details," Barbara admitted with barely detectable distress twenty years later. "I'd bailed several years earlier as his mental illness became serious. The night he died I took the car and drove away into my own life— I became the wild child, doing drugs and going to clubs to blot it out." Her behavior, so seemingly callous, was actually an attempt to keep herself from following him into despair or death, a protective shield of disconnection common in victims of trauma.

But Barbara can flee her past no longer because her children are forcing her to relive it; she has not only a son who resembles her brother but also a daughter, one year younger, who reminds her of herself. She pointed to their picture on her desk at the advertising agency she runs—a serious-looking boy of eight and his far brasher little sister, who has her mother's keen eyes and energetic stance. "I see how reserved he is, and it scares me," she said. "His teacher says he seems depressed and sad. He was so quiet when I took them on vacation recently. My daughter is more like me—I see her repeating the pattern with my son." History seems to be recycling, and she cannot stop the process.

Barbara is terrified of failing her son as she thinks she failed her brother—a universal fear among surviving siblings who become parents. Engulfed in her own tragedy, she cannot distinguish between the responsible parent she now is and the helpless younger sister (with irresponsible parents) she used to be. She does not realize that she has resources as a mature adult that she lacked as an overwhelmed twenty-one-year-old—the power of insight, and the will and courage to explore the horror she has buried for so long. Although she cannot prevent herself from reliving with visceral immediacy what was once unbearable, her relationship with her children offers her an opportunity finally to work through these emotions and lay them to rest.

Like every normal sibling, Barbara must reexperience her own anguish—as well as her guilt, anger and feelings of impotence—to protect her children from the fallout. Then she can discover that a depressed son, with an attuned mother, need not relive the tragedy of a suicidal brother. She needs to identify her compulsion to save her brother retroactively through her son. This could take a variety of forms; she may compensate by overprotecting him or by trying to force her daughter to be more involved with her brother than Barbara was with her own. She should also prepare to experience a wrenching anniversary reaction when her children reach the same ages that she and her brother were when he took his life.

"I don't have a model for how to be a good sibling or parent," Barbara lamented. Fortunately self-knowledge can teach her what she needs to know to be the latter and help her see that her concept of what the former entails was impossible to achieve. The best way to keep her son alive and her daughter sane is to explore her own feelings as fully as possible; the more a normal sibling exposes her hidden past, the less she will act it out.

Having a traumatic sibling relationship is not only a tragedy; it is also an opportunity for insight that can profit the next generation; knowing your vulnerabilities can help you manage them. Maggie Payne, the financial adviser whose refusal to make her hostile sister her maid of honor provoked a fifty-year feud, was determined that her children have a different experience. "The most important thing to me was that my three children be friends and love each other—something I missed all my life," she said, holding back tears. "This still is a tremendous area of sadness for me." She knows that bending over backward to provide a healthier atmosphere in the home she created caused its own problems: "I wasn't allowed to show anger as a child since my sister always did, and it wreaked havoc with my kids—I didn't like them being angry because the hostility was just overwhelming in my house." In her zeal to keep her children from behaving like her sister (and herself), she squelched even their normal aggression. Knowing what she did and why did not entirely prevent Maggie from making mistakes, but it helped her lessen their impact. Her sorrow about the failure of her own sibling relationship is diminished by the pride she takes in helping her children feel love rather than hate for one another.

Just as awareness limits the psychological damage an abnormal sibling causes, obliviousness perpetuates it. Normal siblings who excise all negative feelings toward their own parents tend to treat their children as they themselves were treated; maintaining an air-brushed version of their own family life causes them to oppress their normal children by requiring sacrifices never recognized as such. They demand the same premature maturity that was expected of them and so perpetuate the Caliban Syndrome. Intact siblings who get the subliminal message that they must copy their parents' mode of caretaking in order to be loved pass this attitude on. Becoming their parents' posthumous surrogates vis-à-vis a sibling is a foregone conclusion rather than a considered, difficult decision. A lack of ambivalence about the huge sacrifice that lifelong caring for a seriously debilitated relative entails is always suspect and has repercussions in the next generation.

Paul Morrison is oddly free of resentment toward parents who never figured out what was wrong with his seriously disturbed and disruptive brother, nor got proper treatment or investigated placement for him, let alone considered the impact their abdication had on their healthy son. "My dad assumed that kids were taken away if you pursued aid, and that frightened him, so he didn't do it to avoid a heart-wrenching separation," Paul explained. He discovered only last month, at age thirty-eight, that his brother was actually autistic rather than retarded as he had always thought. "As a kid I just knew he was different, and I never tried to find out why—I took my cue from my parents," he said. He considers his father a model of noble self-sacrifice, ignoring the fact that his behavior irreparably harmed the child he was ostensibly trying to protect.

Paul is still taking his cues from his parents. "I told them at an early age that I'd look after my brother. They put no pressure on me— I was a very responsible little tyke. My life was programmed for this from the beginning," he says matter-of-factly, never wondering who wrote the "program." "I told my wife that he'd always live with me."

A son who feels required to carry out his parents' unexpressed commands to devote his life to his brother's care must deny the severity of the disability and the sacrifice it entails. Even though Paul confessed that his reaction, every time he visits his parents' home, is "Gosh, I thought he was better than this," he feels compelled to recreate the circumstances he grew up in; when informed that good group homes exist for people like his brother, he said, "I don't care to know that." Asked whether spending their childhood with a massively dysfunctional uncle could harm his children, his response was a combination of moral uplift and death wish: "It would broaden them, and maybe I'll outlive him so they won't have to endure it." Like his father, he blinds himself to the toll his resolution will take on everyone involved; being a brother counts more than being a father. Having been made a martyr himself, he intends to make his own children martyrs too.

The problem with Paul's decision is that it is no decision at all but a compulsion that amputates all negative feelings. Had he researched alternatives, consulted his family, and acknowledged the problems they all faced, he could have chosen to have his disabled relative share his home—if he could also afford to make provisions for his brother's care. This would have been a difficult but tolerable situation as long as other members of the family were not coerced into being responsible for his brother at the expense of their own lives and emotions.

Parents need their children to see the world through their eyes; the more disturbing and precariously held the view, the more threatening a contrary perspective can be. Sarah Lattimer is surprised and dismayed that her own three children, all normal, have a more negative attitude toward her deaf-mute, hyperactive, violent sister than she does. She cannot understand why they refused to be counselors at the same camp for the severely handicapped where her parents arranged for her and her two able-bodied siblings to spend every summer as teenagers, or why they are less than enthusiastic about visiting their aunt or taking her out in public. "My parents always encouraged us to take her out, because that's what we're fighting for," Sarah said. "I'd boldly walk her through the grocery store—this was my cause. It's funny that my kids don't have the same attitude; it upsets me."

Sarah's parents were missionaries, whose belief that "God has selected our family as a special place for Mary" helped them cope with the tragedy of their eldest child's massive disabilities. Although Sarah insists she "didn't miss out on childhood," she described scenes that would try a saint—hours of daily caretaking that took her away from extracurricular activities, never being allowed to have friends over, forgoing all family outings and celebrations, having no claim on her parents' attention. "They were advocates for accepting that this was your lot in life," Sarah explained uncomplainingly. The Lattimers' attitude sanctified their sacrifices, but also made it inconceivable—even sinful—for their daughter to object to being saturated in a culture of disability. A daughter who is emmeshed in her parents' view of the world expects nothing less of her own children.

Sarah thinks of her own family as a continuation of her childhood experience; "We're a family of five, just as my family was," she noted. She too is deeply religious and, like her parents, considers herself an advocate of "this is your lot in life." When her children express what she was forbidden even to feel, she becomes anxious and uncomfortable and is likely to communicate more displeasure than she realizes. Although she insists—and truly believes—that she "puts the children first," she is also convinced that carrying on the Lattimer family mission to put her sister first is a fundamental and universal moral duty.

Sarah embraces her family's attitude unquestioningly and wants to recapitulate it; ironically, a pattern can repeat itself even when a healthy sibling bends over backward to repudiate a parent's behavior, often in ways that the sibling fails to recognize. When Jane London discovered that one of her daughters had a serious stuttering problem, she was determined never to turn the child into a helpless invalid as her mother had done with her socially awkward sister; she also resolved that her normal daughter would never be saddled with a troublesome sister as she herself had been. She is keenly aware that her own mother—an unhappy and isolated woman—had always identified with and preferred her sister. "My impaired daughter has the same coloring as her aunt, whom my parents treated as a frail, damaged kid," Jane said. "So I never let her say, 'This is hard for me,' because I didn't want her to feel entitled to whine or be a weakling. I didn't want her to be a cripple like my parents made my sister."

These motives seem rational and in the child's interest, but there is another, less conscious, and more harmful side; in her fervor to protect her healthy daughter from being "shortchanged," Jane shows as clear a preference for one child over the other as her own mother did, rejecting and criticizing her struggling daughter in favor of the one who, like herself, "does well." It is embarrassing for her to admit that she prefers the child who resembles her; she would be shocked to realize that she is behaving much more like her mother than she ever intended.

Relationships with damaged siblings reverberate through many generations, including those not yet born. When normal children become parents, they may find to their dismay that by trying to avoid one kind of trouble, they have caused another.

Issues provoked by damaged siblings have affected at least three generations of women in the Goodman family. Cindy Goodman was the invisible sister whose older brother was not only physically deformed by a cleft palate but was also brilliant and was preferred by her mother for both reasons. All her life she felt that her claims to attention "never measured up" to either his abilities or his disabilities. When Cindy became the mother of a schizophrenic son and a younger unimpaired daughter—replicating her own family constellation—she was determined that her daughter not suffer the same fate. "I paid lots of attention because with me none was paid," Cindy said. "My parents were so lacking in compassion for me. I have to make sure that just because my daughter's not handicapped her life is as important as my son's." She showed empathy and concern to preserve her daughter Amy's autonomy, repeating several times that she "must pay attention" to her. The attention included shielding Amy from the worst details of her brother's psychotic episodes. "I keep her appraised of what's happening with him, but I don't go into specifics so as not to diminish her own experience—I turn to friends instead," she explained, demonstrating rare sensitivity and self-control in dreadful circumstances. Cindy is proud of the independence and self-esteem that she has fostered in Amy. "She is so much different from me—and I like that," she said.

I got a dizzyingly different picture from Amy, who is thirty-five and pregnant with her third child. According to her, Cindy had indeed avoided making her invisible—and had made her feel perversely preeminent instead. Her guilt, her resentment, and her oppressive sense that she is responsible for her mother's emotional stability is intense and utterly unsuspected by Cindy. Amy agreed that attention was paid, but only so that she could focus on Cindy, who, having been ignored by her own mother, needed to be the real center of attention for her daughter. Their mothers' demands may have diverged, but Amy, like Cindy before her, feels she never measures up to them. Though the mother and daughter do differ, some of their underlying issues are identical.

Amy knows how crushing Cindy's centrality in her life—and how conditional her love—has felt. "I always thought it was my responsibility to take care of her emotionally, to make up for my brother," she said, "and I was always afraid she'd cut off contact if I didn't please her. I worry about how every decision I make will affect her, like I have no right to do anything independently."

Recently Cindy has been making a particularly onerous demand on Amy—one she never mentioned to me. "She's putting blatant pressure on me to move back home, constantly sending my husband job announcements," Amy said. Since she already visits home more frequently than she wants to and has no desire to live there, opposing her mother's wishes is trying her sorely: "I've needed to be physically present, to make up for what he can't provide—who else does she have? I have her only grandchildren. I've felt like an only child."

Amy is still struggling to separate from Cindy, but meanwhile she too is determined to pay attention to her own children's needs as hers were not; bearing the burden of her mother's happiness without the support of her only sibling makes her want to guarantee that her children do not suffer the same fate—so she has conceived a spare sibling for them. "It would really have been nice to have had another brother or sister and not feel as isolated as I did when he got sick," she explained. "There seems to be lots of support among siblings. Having three will be better for them because they'll feel less pressure—I want that for my kids." So intent is she to retroactively remedy her own life that she cannot imagine that even her idyllic solution could create other problems. Her children, despite her efforts, may never be as close as she desires. She could unduly favor the "insurance policy" baby who represents the perfect sibling she herself wanted to rely on, or reject it if it fails to meet her expectations; assigning a role to a child in utero, irrelevant to its actual qualities and realities that are always different from yours, is a tricky business. And Cindy may have more of a sense of how her own history is getting played out than she realizes; despite her sincere desire to "protect the next generation," she confessed to me, "I tried not to recreate my own family, but in some ways I did it anyway."

Some normal siblings, like Maggie and Cindy, go to any lengths not to repeat their parents' errors; others, like Paul and Sarah, think their parents made none. Like Barbara, all of them dread seeing their damaged siblings' faces reflected in the faces of their own children—and they always will. Their fear is a deflected manifestation of the fear of contagion, a symptom of the Caliban Syndrome. How can they limit the extent to which they pass Caliban on?

Accepting that to some degree you are inexorably bound to reproduce at least part of the essence if not the form of your original family relationships, and not only in ways you consciously choose (or wish), is a crucial step. This involves giving up the grandiose notion that you can change history. No human being can control everything—the unconscious is particularly recalcitrant to such efforts—but self-knowledge gives you a huge advantage. Question your own agenda, inquire into your own motivation, and do not expect your children to fix your past. Above all, listen to your children and be aware of the universal tendency to fit them into molds and roles that meet your needs rather than theirs. Think about the impact your sibling has on you and how your parents dealt with each of you, including hidden dimensions; pay special attention to what you do not want to know. The deeper your knowledge of your own past relationships with Caliban, as the secret repository of your hopes and fears, the less you and future generations will be condemned to repeat them.

PART III

A Life
of One's
Own

chapter 10

My Brother's Keeper

"WHO WILL TAKE CARE of my brother when my parents are dead?" is the question, literal or metaphoric, that haunts every normal sibling. From the able-bodied brother who refuses to work to the mentally impaired sister who neither sees nor speaks, abnormal siblings provoke soul-searching in their kin. If her disability is incapacitating, should you institutionalize her, pay for her care, or let her move in with you? If your relationship with him has been aversive since childhood, must you maintain at least minimal contact simply because he is your closest relative or because your mother asked you to? What degree of involvement does conscience require and convenience permit? Try as you may, you can never simply forget about such a sibling. Must you be your brother's keeper, however *keeping* is defined? Even asking the question makes you suspect; after all, Cain had already murdered his brother Abel when he asked it of God.

Guilt is rarely absent from the thoughts of healthy adults about their damaged siblings because no amount of devotion or care can make the damaged whole or blot out the dark victory of their own normality. Expectations of parents and a sense of duty, as well as love, compassion, and ignorance of humane alternatives, cause some to assume excessive responsibility for siblings in dire need; the "blood is thicker than water" mentality binds others even to those they dislike and do not have to care for directly.

Whether they embrace caretaking as a mission or categorically refuse it; whether they struggle with the conflict between theirs and the other's needs or make an uneasy truce, siblings of the abnormal are forced by accidents of fate to deal with a dilemma that nobody else has to think about. Contact with them can run the gamut from the occasional check or strained phone call to around-the-clock tending. Intact siblings are never free from worry or self-recrimination no matter what they do; those who insist that they were "programmed for this [total responsibility] from the beginning" doubt themselves as much as those who assert that "I would kill myself or him if I had to take him in." These concerns rarely get discussed because they seem so shameful.

Years before they are likely to be called on to take over caring for their seriously disabled siblings as their parents expect them to do, Jack Morelli and Sandy Wilson are losing sleep over their anticipated burden. How will they recreate the carefully constructed environments in which their misguided but dedicated parents have cocooned their fragile children? How could they refuse to try?

When I asked Jack, a thirty-four-year-old actor, about his reclusive older sister Margaret's fate after his parents' death, his voice trembled with anxiety. "Oh my God, that's all I think about," he told me. "I've lain awake nights starting at age thirteen worrying—what is she going to do?" Worrying about what he is going to do with her causes Jack even more insomnia; Margaret, whose condition has never been diagnosed, dropped out of high school and has lived with her parents ever since: her only short stint working—in a fast-food restaurant—came to a devastating end when the other employees locked her in the basement as a practical joke. "She spends her life in isolation, watching TV and collecting artifacts from 1963," Jack said, equally cognizant of the pity and annoyance she evokes in him. "She ruins everything at home. My parents tolerate this—that's the way they cope. Only in my twenties did I realize that they're part of it, that her situation is their fault; she gives my mother a sense of purpose, and my parents think that by spoiling her, they're providing for her. When I try to talk to them about her future, they say, 'God will take care of her.' How can they say that? Everything is so regimented—how can I reproduce it? I worry that this fragile house of cards will topple."

Instead of resenting his parents for designating him God's factotum, Jack worries about recreating a protected atmosphere for Margaret. But by refusing to discuss or to plan for their daughter's future beyond naïve assertions of faith, they abdicate their responsibilities toward both their children—an all-too-common scenario.

Although Jack admitted that this plan might be "too hopeful," he thought he might be able to install Margaret in an apartment down the street and pay her bills. Like many intact siblings, he intermittently denies the full extent of his sister's disability and minimizes the amount of care she requires because he cannot stand the implications for his own life; to know the truth would make him feel even more guilty, anxious, and angry. It is also hard for him to take a stand against his parents' implicit wishes and refuse to take over for them. "I feel inextricably bound to them all, and I wish I didn't," he says. "We'll probably have to live together someday, so I wouldn't want to have a child—it would be another person to be responsible for. Other people don't have to worry about this as young adults." There was, though, a glimmer of possibility beyond resigning himself to a life as constricted as his sister's: "I have to learn to realize that even if I move to South America they won't combust." Jack also has to learn that they won't combust if he lives in this country either.

"I saw an article in the paper about the three issues we normal siblings face," said twenty-seven-year-old Sandy, whose brain-damaged, paranoid older brother Michael cannot hold a job and refused to move into an apartment his parents found for him because the Disney Channel was not available there. "First it's making friends and bringing them home, then it's romance, and then it's aging parents. I feel like a statistic—my course is plotted till I'm sixty!" The course Sandy claustrophobically foresees leaves no room for her own wishes; she already stifles them, ostensibly to avoid Michael's jealousy. "My parents won't consider an institution, and they don't plan for the future," she told me. "My mother constantly asks me to reassure her—'You'll take care of him, won't you?' It's definitely expected. I'm forced to accept their agenda, or I'd be letting everyone down." The tension in Sandy's voice, in her slight body and prematurely serious expression, is palpable as she speaks, stifling sobs; she seems almost physically weighted down by a fate that is as unbearable as it is inescapable.

Most normal children are so caught up in their own guilt and their parents' blinkered expectations that they never question what is actually in the best interest of the disabled; to consider other options besides providing care themselves seems selfish and cruel.

Sandy, however, charges that devoting her life to her brother would not only oppress her but isolate him. Unlike Jack, she recognizes the severity of her sibling's problems. "My parents have an image of him and an image of me, both of which are actually their projection. I've suggested for years that he should be with other brain-injured people, and they refuse, but when he went to a group on his own, he enjoyed it. They are denying him his peers; he's more social than they are, and less functional than they think he is. Why is our culture so group home–phobic?"

Other intact siblings express little of the ambivalence or angst that oppresses Sandy and Jack. Religious faith, moral codes, filial or fraternal devotion—as well as less lofty motives like self-punishment or avoiding other relationships—prompt them to regard caretaking as their mission in life. They are guardians and proud of it.

Sarah Lattimer's attitude toward directing her massively handicapped sister Mary's care is so low-key that she wondered if her story was relevant to this book. "I'm a matter-of-fact person," she explained, "so when it fell in my lap, I surprised myself by rising to the occasion." With a combination of denial and calm acceptance, this daughter of missionaries says, "I don't feel it's had a tremendous impact on my life because it's just another thing—other people have fathers who travel all the time. My approach comes from my faith; I have to step up to it." Her religious convictions, as well as her identification with her own parents and her ability to suppress the natural ambivalence of anyone facing this burden, contribute to Sarah's "oh well, that's the way it is" mode of coping with Mary.

Compassion, culturally defined responsibilities, and unresolved emotional conflicts have caused Susan Kim to take up the role as her retarded brother's live-in guardian with a vengeance. "I'm the eldest daughter in a Korean family," said this successful but sorrowful businesswoman. "It's shameful to think you wouldn't want that responsibility, and I don't believe in doing anything half-assed." More than duty or perfectionism binds her to her brother: "My relationship with him is the best of everybody in the family. I'm not a patient person, but with him I am more so than with my normal siblings. It's a conscious effort on my part to be, and to work at being, understanding, open, and tolerant. You have to be thoughtful and respectful; check your ego at the door." Being self-effacing and steadfast for her brother is an important source of Susan's self-esteem; she prides herself on taking better care of Sam than their mother ever did. "I hired a teacher to help him, something she never thought to do," she said.

Susan does acknowledge, as Sarah does not, that her exertions take a toll: "My weight goes up and down, and the stress is physically manifested in rashes. I go home exhausted from always trying to do the right thing. It's the curse of being who you are—otherwise I wouldn't be proud of myself." She assumes that her herculean efforts are required because her brother would not flourish without them. In a group home, she is convinced, "he'd be miserable, locked up like an animal and drugged." There is something both grim and gallant in her uncompromising stance.

Many people assume that the only alternative to sacrificing their lives to care for damaged siblings is imprisoning them in a place like the Willowbrook Developmental Center, the huge, notorious institution for the retarded in Staten Island where, a 1972

exposé revealed, incontinent children were kept in pens like ani-
mals. In fact, most people I spoke to whose handicapped siblings
live in the smaller group homes that now predominate praised their
warm environments and caring staffs. "My brother has never been
happier," they said. Finding the right setting is still not easy, but at
least now it is often possible.

Concern for her brother's welfare and misinformation about
community resources are not the only reasons Susan tends him at
huge personal cost; her role as his protector provides her with an
unassailably noble rationale for avoiding an intimate relationship
with a peer. "Whomever I would choose would also have to be
unusually patient and understanding to be involved with my
brother," she insists, "and I haven't met anybody compassionate
enough to even ask them the question." Caring for him serves her
needs as much as his.

Living with a relative who needs constant attention is an
engrossing and onerous responsibility that should never be under-
taken without serious consideration of the consequences for your
life and for those you love; no one should agree to it automatically.
The motives of those who do take it on are never purely altruistic.
Guardians usually have a hidden agenda—pleasing (or not disappointing) parents, deflecting intimacy, expiating guilt and hostility,
structuring their own lives. Recognizing these normal feelings
makes you a better caretaker, one less likely to inappropriately
enlist others in the effort and more able to take care of yourself.

"I don't envy people whose parents don't plan," said Jackie Hanson, whose parents finally placed her homework-eating autistic sister Joan in a group home where she is "not unhappy." Jackie chose to
become Joan's guardian after working through her intense feelings

about her sister, with whom she had been psychically merged throughout childhood. "I visit once a month," she told me, "and it feels fine and voluntary, whereas before it felt like an obligation. Dealing with our relationship changed that; we're very close now." With luck and hard emotional work, it is possible to become a loving caretaker who is neither oblivious nor a martyr.

Sometimes, however, the only way to care for yourself is to refuse to care for someone else; working through intense feelings about the person does not necessarily make a good relationship possible. Not everyone can be, or should be, a brother's keeper. When siblings are overwhelming, abusive, relentlessly irresponsible, or simply unbearable, disengagement is the only prudent course of action—though rarely a conflict-free one for a brother or sister. "I can't ruin the family that I'm building," said a woman whose crushing guilt about her choice caused her to flee the country with her husband and child. Nonetheless, repudiating your responsibility for such a sibling can be self-affirming and in the interest of the impaired person.

Katie Clark's relationship with her volatile autistic brother was so aversive that she went to college three thousand miles away—a common ploy to create emotional distance from a problem sibling through geographic distance. "Staying home and having to deal with him made me panic," she said. When she returned, she reconsidered the foregone conclusion that she would take over his care—a role she had always dreaded but felt compelled to accept. Four years of separation gave her another perspective and altered how she defined both her duty and her brother's welfare. "I've distanced myself from my family even though I now live only an hour from them," Katie said. "Being away at college and talking to people there made me realize that support doesn't have to come from relatives. I can't maintain my own sanity and be his caretaker, although acting on this conviction induces a lot of guilt. People know what they can handle—if you know you can't and you do it anyway, you're doing a disservice to the other person. I wonder whether my parents are wrong to have my brother live at home—he might be better off if they found a residence. Since I've been back, I've talked to other people in my situation, and it's been a revelation how much happier a sibling can be there. This hadn't occurred to me before."

Charlotte MacDonald's very life depended on her declining guardianship for the violent, epileptic brother who had tried to strangle her when she was six. "At age nine," she said, "I made a pact with myself that if they made me come back and take care of him, I would kill myself." After her mother died several years later—her life shortened, Charlotte is certain, by the rigors of caring for her son—Charlotte prevailed on her father to find placement for him. This move, necessitated by tragic circumstances, proved the salvation of both siblings. "He's more functional than he's ever been," Charlotte said with palpable relief. "The staff at the home is very good, and we don't have to worry about what's going to happen when my father dies." Guardianship should never be an option when it would imperil the designated guardian's physical or psychological survival. It is no crime for your own life to come first.

In addition to yielding to family pressure or working out their own psychic conflicts, many siblings maintain masochistic relationships with impossible relatives because they confuse setting boundaries with abandoning the desperate. Even when they manage to cut off contact, they take the blame if the person self-destructs; guilt is always waiting in the wings.

After Nathan Kingsley's unsocialized borderline sister died of a drug overdose, he never forgave himself for setting limits with her. "Ten years ago I told her not to visit any more," said Nathan, displaying the portfolio of pictures of his sister that he carried everywhere. "She was so surly, nasty, and mean. I said, 'Stay away if you're not going to be decent.' I'd set her up in college, but she never could make a go of it—she fancied herself a radio star or a beauty queen. She was so different from everyone else in the family. My parents turned over their entire lives to her." Like his parents, Nathan made every effort to help his miserable and provocative sister, whose life was a revolving door of treatment programs, prostitution, and drug addiction, until he banished her because of her effect on his own children. "Dee Dee—she made up this name for herself—used to spend every New Year's with us, but being around her became too uncomfortable." Despite his sensible course of action, Nathan torments himself for letting his sister down. "I cut myself off from her—I could have done more," he said wretchedly. "I gave her refuge and never let her come back to it. I think I could have turned her around, and I ignored her." In his anguish Nathan fails to realize that his fantasy of saving Dee Dee makes him as grandiose as she was. Instead of punishing himself from being a heartless brother, he should commend himself for being a responsible father.

Children are not only the beneficiaries but frequently the agents who liberate their parents from sibling bondage; ironically, they most often serve this function for parents who promised their own parents that they would be caretakers for life. The "be nice to your poor sister" refrain does not stop in adulthood or even when the supplicants are dead. Since children suffer the consequences of chronic exposure to noxious aunts or uncles, they have legitimate grievances that parents can sometimes recognize more easily than their own travails. Children provide a jolt of reality, a fresh perspective, and a justification for a course of action that their elders would feel too guilty to pursue for themselves alone.

"My mother's biggest fear was that I wouldn't take care of my sister," said boutique owner Mimi Newhouse. "But why should I take care of a grown woman?" Mimi's sister—who had returned clothes she borrowed to Mimi's closet covered with pizza and overturned Mimi's fully set table at Thanksgiving—has not improved with age. Despite resentment that "she never got it together and can't keep a job," Mimi's sense of obligation (and residual discomfort about her own prosperity) made her periodically bail her sister out. "When I let her work in my store, she answered the phone with an edge in her voice and alienated my customers and employees." She also alienated Mimi's daughter, the manager. "My daughter said, 'It's her or me,' and then I finally fired her," said Mimi, with a combination of guilt and gratitude. "My mother left me my sister—and she reminds me of my mother. She makes me feel responsible. Why is this so hard?"

Disconnecting from taking care of an impossible sibling is so hard because it feels like you are betraying the parental trust that differentiated you from that sibling in the first place. Though parents may think otherwise, siblings have less responsibility for damaged siblings than their parents do—and parents would make arrangements if they had no normal offspring to rely on. From within a family it can be difficult to see that a sibling should not automatically come first, before your children, your spouse, your profession, or yourself.

Norman Albee calculates that he has given his wayward sister

$100,000 over the years, to no avail. He paid for her divorce, for her mortgage to prevent the bank from foreclosing on her house, and for a lawyer to keep her out of jail when she helped her daughter kidnap her own daughter, and he did it all without ever being thanked, at his mother's behest. "Everything was for my mother's peace of mind, because she asked me to look out for my sister after she died," said the dutiful son, now seventy years old. "We used to dread the phone calls. She's like a millstone trying to drag me under—you sink, but she'll survive." His own daughter saved his peace of mind by insisting he stop intervening; it took her thirty years to convince him. "She realized we'd had enough of my sister, and eventually I stopped taking her calls," he said, relieved that his daughter gave him permission to disobey his long-dead mother.

Recognizing that you have no control over a sibling's behavior, when that behavior has disastrous consequences, is horrendously difficult even if no parent is expecting you to remain involved. Janice Becker, who had fished her mentally ill sister out of the river, gravely accepted the truth. "There's nothing I can do. I can't bring her home and let the cycle start all over again with her stopping her medication. I feel anger because she is where she is and I am where I am, but no guilt, because everything I've got I've worked for—I tried to help above and beyond." Though Janice was rational and resolute, she still had tears in her eyes when she described seeing her sister, obese and in rags, begging for food in front of the church they had attended together as children. Even when guilt is gone, grief remains.

Lisa Masterson stopped "soup to nuts caretaking," including paying for her cocaine-addicted brother's rent and countless drug treatment programs, when his therapist instructed her to do so.

"It's the hardest thing to see him in pain, but no matter what I did, he was still in pain," she concluded. Fortunately, she found a way to fulfill her destiny as a "genetically engineered caretaker" by assisting those who could profit from her intervention: she helps raise the three children he fathered with three different mothers.

A sibling does not have to be flamboyantly or publicly dysfunctional to try the patience of his brothers and sisters and provoke them to sever the tie out of self-protection. Set designer Jim Brown's younger brother Dan started bouncing checks in college. In the subsequent thirty years Jim loaned Dan money, found him employment ("His attitude and ethics were such that they let him go—I felt bad for him and that I'd recommended him"), and encouraged him to go on interviews ("When I suggest anything, he screams at me"), but he never kept a job. Dan finally moved back into their mother's apartment, content to let her support him. "He doesn't want to work," Jim said bitterly. "It would take away from his time on the computer. He uses diabetes as an excuse now, but I have it too. Why should he depend on an elderly woman?"

Jim has come to realize that it is pointless or worse to try to assist his brother. "There's nothing I can do to make the situation better, and nothing I should do. You have to be able to talk and for the person to see there's a problem. I'd like to feel there's some way to help my brother and my mother, but I've given up trying. If I had to pay my rent, I'd dig a ditch, but he's guaranteed food and a roof, so why should he bother? My mother hasn't the strength to kick him out."

Once again an unresolved sibling issue in a parent's past reappears: "It's psychological backlash. My mother feels guilty for her own brother's actions—he abandoned his pregnant wife and never

151

saw their son, so she has to bend over backward to be the antithesis of what he was."

Jim has dealt with his disappointment by distancing himself from his brother and mother's unhealthy relationship. "I used to care for him," he told me, "but I've stopped. I told both of them I would not support him after her death." He calls this technique "pain management" : "I've lived with physical pain, and I work not to let it affect me. I compartmentalize that part of my life. This is psychological pain. It's really upsetting, so I try not to think about it, but I wouldn't be surprised if I'd put it somewhere where it's another color, another pressure. If I dwelled on it, I'd get depressed."

Jim's approach, while it takes considerable energy and is only moderately effective, is preferable to the harm he would do by implicitly condoning his brother's sponging. When coping with a troubled and troubling sibling, damage control is often the best you can do.

One way normal siblings deal with their often hopeless desire to make a difference to their damaged sibling is to generalize it by joining a helping profession; they are overrepresented in the ranks of therapists, doctors, nurses, and advocates and educators of the disabled. The pull to pursue these careers is so strong that one woman protested that she resented the assumption that she would "sign up" as a special ed teacher, as though she naturally fit the hereditary job description. Even then she could not entirely escape; she ended up writing books about therapy rather than conducting it herself.

"Ninety percent of my career choice was Johnny," said social work student Samantha Greenberg. Life with her oppositional, "extremely low IQ" brother had sensitized her to the plight of the disabled, and she decided to dedicate her professional life to helping people like him. But Samantha also expected to devote her private life to helping her brother; she is another dutiful sibling to whom it never occurred that there was any other option. "I always assumed his place should be with me and that whoever I'd marry would have to understand," she said, "until the other students in my class said, 'You're going to take this on?' They made me realize it's not something you automatically have to do."

Samantha's fellow students enlightened her both personally and professionally. "Before they questioned me, I thought, 'Who else is going to do it?' I felt a real family sense of duty; in a helping profession you don't do much asking about your own feelings. But now I'm considering the impact on my own family—and what if he wants to get married too?" The "revelation" she came to with her colleagues' assistance will be in the interest of Samantha's future family, as well as in the interest of the families she will counsel from a newly broadened perspective.

Although a career as a symbolic caretaker meets the needs of many normal siblings, it can also represent an oppressive continuation of the role forced upon them as too-responsible, prematurely mature children. Coming into your own may require leaving the profession as well as rejecting that role in private life.

Rebecca Ashford left social work and simultaneously cut off contact with her unmanageable learning-disabled brother when she realized that both "jobs" were making her miserable. "My profession was entirely determined by my position in my family," said Rebecca, who is now an illustrator. "My family was such a burden to me and always came to me as a mediator; I was in charge of my brother since I was sixteen years old, when my mother got cancer. I fought all his battles. He was an albatross around my neck. Social work was a continuation of that role in the rest of my life; helping is what I do—and I choose not to do it twenty-four hours a day anymore."

Rebecca had never questioned her life's work until recently. "It was all just obligation, and I didn't know it," she said. Nonetheless, even though Rebecca knows that she is making healthy choices, she plagues herself with recriminations on both fronts: "I no longer want the responsibility, but leaving social work was guilt-provoking; I couldn't shake the depression. I feel terrible that I can take care of everyone else but can't be there for my own brother. But I put in my years, and I'm paroled." Though she set herself free, Rebecca still feels like a criminal.

The most common reason siblings assume responsibility for abnormal relatives is to carry on what they believe is a family tradition of caring. In a surprisingly large number of cases, however, healthy children feel that they must remain involved with a brother or sister at no matter what personal cost precisely because their parents did not care.

"I couldn't live with myself if I abandoned my brother like our parents abandoned us," said Pam Lewis, a lawyer whose paranoid schizophrenic brother broke down her office door and presented a penis-shaped nutcracker to her young daughters. "I said to him, 'Our parents didn't do right by us, so let's make a pledge that we'll always be there for each other.'" Pam is frightened and repelled by her brother, who has been arrested for stalking, but she forces herself to maintain contact as an act of "fraternal obligation." "If I never saw him again as long as I live, I wouldn't care," she admitted. "I have no particular love for him and I don't even like him, but I have a responsibility to do all that's possible simply because he's my brother. I feel sorry for him—to reject him would make me a bad person. We were both rejected all our lives, so I'm sensitive to this; I've got to help him." But fraternal duty is not the only obligation in life: "Recently I've felt less anxious to be the good sister because he's becoming increasingly violent. I can't endanger and sacrifice myself or my children. In what degree am I my brother's keeper?"

Pam's question is inescapable, even for those who did not face the wrenching decision about whether to provide direct care. Siblings berate themselves relentlessly for what they feel as much as for how they behave; no matter how much they are provoked, they cannot forgive themselves for lacking proper brotherly or sisterly love. Shame and guilt about neglecting or rejecting a damaged sibling pursue them like furies.

Guilt-assuaging outings are a popular way to make restitution. Susan Kim steels herself for the week-long fishing trip with her retarded brother that she schedules annually. Political scientist Randy Lane was sickened by the intense relief he felt when he moved to a distant city and could no longer take his Tourette's-afflicted brother to the local amusement park "Every year, onerously, we used to go for the whole day, but it got too mortifying," he admitted. Randy can hardly bear his dual feelings of contempt and revulsion for his brother and for himself: "I blame myself for not doing more for him, especially since my father won't even go to fucking dinner with him." He feels like a failure as a human being because he lacks "the wonderful ability that some people, like the group home staff, have to not let it affect them at all." When I point out that compassion can be far easier to feel for someone who is not your brother, Randy says shamefacedly, "I should feel more because he is."

Those who cannot tolerate direct contact substitute the guilt-assuaging check. "I give gifts of money to all four of my brothers," said the only one who is not in jail; "it's empowering." In addition to providing occasional financial relief for his family members, this gesture reaffirms his superiority to them, which is always in doubt. But even hearing a sibling's voice is too much for some people; however obligated she feels, Diana Lamm cannot bring herself to return her psychopathic brother's birthday messages on her answering machine. "I know I should call him back," Diana says, "but I think of five million things I have to do including scrubbing the basement floor, so I can't. I ask myself if I should be taking care of him. Even if I wanted to, I don't know if I could. I'm so dissociated from him, he's like a stranger. It's almost like my brother's gone already." Like virtually everyone I interviewed, Diana never told her therapist—or anyone but her husband—about these feelings.

"I could pick up the phone, but he's so irritating," Rebecca Ashford said. "My brother has a way of grating on your nerves—a simple conversation is nails on a blackboard. I can't handle the frustration; I have no patience." Despite everything Rebecca did to assist him, she continues to blame herself for how he makes her feel. "The big unresolved issue I'll take to my grave is my failure as a sister. If only I could stand to make him feel like he has somebody, that he could talk to me once a week—he wasn't loved by my father. I used to wonder how I could stand to invite him if I got married, so I've decided I won't have a wedding."

Candy Fine, the pregnant copywriter who is so horrified at the prospect of dealing with her paranoid brother for the rest of her life that she is moving her family to France, despises herself for what she believes is cold cowardice. "When he was in the hospital, I went every single day. It was only twenty minutes away—I felt so guilty if I didn't that I couldn't live with myself."

Candy voiced a secret worry that afflicts the majority of normal siblings: "Do I love him because he's my brother, because he's a good person, or because I'm supposed to? I can't tell because I'm afraid it's the latter—and I don't want to think about it too much. If it were true, I'd be sorry for him—he needs people to love him, and he's not that lovable. This question comes to mind when it shouldn't—I feel so guilty that I can't sleep with my husband."

As in the biblical story, the normal ones are marked like Cain, doomed by sibling thought-murders to roam the world without respite. Their punishment is never to be permitted unadulterated joy.

chapter 11

The Caliban Syndrome I: Repudiation and Identification

THE CALIBAN SYNDROME AFFECTS every normal child—the invisible and the preeminent, the caretaker and the estranged, the insistent denier and the painfully conscious are all equally prone to it. Damaged siblings lodge deeply in the psyche, where they leave indelible marks on intimate relationships, even with the unborn.

Caliban is the sibling image that normal ones carry within, a potent fantasy derived from actual experiences, parental attitudes, and personal interpretations, that silently shapes the self.

The four symptoms of this syndrome affect everyone differently, but no one escapes:

premature maturity

Normal children grow up too fast. They are expected to shoulder too much responsibility for their siblings and themselves without complaint. As a result, they substitute spurious autonomy for "childish" dependency. If they internalize their parents' standards, they become masochistic and strangers to their own needs.

survivor guilt

Normal children are tormented by being (as well as relieved to be) forever better off than their siblings. They never feel fully entitled to happiness or power. Every achievement is tainted because it occurs in the shadow of one who can never compete. Knowledge of their undeserved advantages makes them prone to anxiety, self-sabotage, and the excruciating grandiose notion that any success of theirs exacerbates their sibling's failure.

compulsion to achieve

Normal children must succeed for two, both to compensate their parents for having a child who cannot fulfill their dreams, and to prove their own superiority and worthiness to themselves—qualities that are always in doubt. The pressure they feel breeds perfectionism, inordinate fear of failure, and the inability to relax and enjoy life.

fear of contagion

Dread of magically catching the disability plagues normal siblings. This fantasy originates in guilt that they were spared and shame that they have more in common with the damaged one than they want to admit. It leads to hypervigilance for signs of damage within the self and the secret conviction that normality is tenuous or a sham.

FEAR OF CONTAGION, the most insidious symptom of the Caliban Syndrome, has paradoxical manifestations: either repudiation or identification with the damaged sibling. The former—the course I chose—is a phobic attempt to excise the other's presence from your life or psyche; the latter is merger with the damaged one. Either you think you have nothing in common with the sibling, or everything.

In contrast, acknowledgment—the insight Prospero attains at the end of *The Tempest* when he says of Caliban, "this thing of darkness I/acknowledge mine"—integrates both repudiation and identification into the self. Normal siblings must feel the power of the Caliban Syndrome in order to transform it.

repudiation

"My sister is my model of what not to be" is a common, and frequently conscious, refrain for normal ones. Many devote their lives to what one called "setting myself in opposition." Striving to become, and to maintain yourself, as "not my sibling"—not fat, not friendless, not lazy, not crazy—is motivated by dread that the undesirable traits will "rub off" on you. Fear of contagion is so compelling that it even affects those whose siblings have genetic defects that they do not share; plenty of intellectuals worry about "waking up retarded like my brother." Whether contagion is impossible (no one acquires attention deficit disorder), unlikely (few sighted people go blind), or inevitable (everyone feels depressed on occasion), the source of the anxiety is being related biologically and psychologically to a damaged sibling.

In the dynamics that underlie *The Tempest*, Miranda needs to make sure everything Caliban-like within her stays in Caliban. Therefore she suppresses her lust, her hostility, and her yearning for independence—everything that is not what her father needs her to be. In the play she simply feels none of these things; in real life Mirandas have to work at it.

Molding yourself into the opposite of a problem sibling, the most common form of repudiation, creates a cordon sanitaire around the too-close-for-comfort catastrophe of the other's life. Externalizing the damage keeps the defects safely deposited in the sibling. But walls of psychic separation are hard to build and require constant maintenance. They are also never entirely impregnable.

Art historian Bob Mansfield is riveted by the numbers on his bathroom scale. Despite his striking presence, dashing wardrobe, and fine physique—which he spends three hours a day at the gym perfecting—he insists he has "no concept of how I look. It's a blind spot, even after thirty years of therapy." In an attempt to "always appear exactly the same at any given moment in public," Bob, a gourmet who also managed restaurants, has maintained his weight at precisely 168 pounds for years, "never deviating or fluctuating"; "I don't eat a lot," he said. A three-hundred-pound sister who is only one year younger ("we were sort of like twins") is the negative inspiration for this exacting regimen. "She's a constant reminder of what to not let happen—I say, 'I have none of that,' he explained. "I'm afraid of not being attractive and the limitation that that would present; I'm self-conscious about my weight to this very minute."

Although Bob is clearly aware that his single-minded pursuit of svelteness is a reaction to his sister's obesity, he does not link his compulsive exactitude with her; only when I pursued the topic did he remark that his sister was not only hugely fat but that her weight "fluctuated wildly." Nor did he relate his need to be a "model of self-discipline who feels pressure never to fail at anything" to his sister's abdication of self-control. Most importantly, this otherwise insightful man missed the common element in their characters: food rules them both. Obsession with embodying the opposite of a sibling always has its unconscious side.

A brother who is immobilized by despair is the cautionary example for publicist Karen James. "I don't like to be depressed," she said. "I want to get past it as quickly as possible. When I'm upset, I try to distract myself." Karen works so hard not to be paralyzed that she throws herself into activity; she forced herself to go out dancing the night she broke up with her boyfriend. "I realize how much my behavior has been defined by my brother," she says. Karen's technique, which in moderation would be a sensible antidote to inertia, is excessive and desperate. Any feeling that must be automatically neutralized because of sibling resonances can never be worked through.

"I'm in charge," asserts Dana Thompson. "I've worked so hard to become competent because I'm the only sane one in the family." Dana's whiny, self-involved, barely functional older sister—whom she already dreads having to spend holidays with after their mother dies—is her negative model. When her sister suggested that they were alike, Dana recoiled in horror: "I wanted to shout, 'I'm nothing like you, don't mistake this'"—a judgment she would not have had to deny so vociferously if she did not fear it was correct. Dana finds herself inordinately disturbed by any intimation of incompetence, however trivial. "I felt surprisingly defensive when the baby-sitter criticized my housekeeping," she said. "I know how hard I've worked to be different, but I never talked about this in therapy. There's much more here than I think about."

Those who insist that they are the absolute antithesis of a damaged brother or sister are always suspect; they behave as though admitting the slightest commonality would contaminate them. When asked what he had in common with the psychopathic sister he had bailed out financially for years, Norman Albee categorically dismissed the notion. "It's a night-and-day situation—we're two completely different personalities," he said huffily. "There is no emotional connection at all." He claimed that filial duty alone had prompted his largesse, which had stopped only when his daughter intervened; in fact, his need to demonstrate his superiority and underscore the differences had also prevented him from extricating himself from this oppressive obligation sooner.

"Do I see my brother in myself? Not in the least," Jim Brown responded to my inquiry. Jim, who had finally given up trying to find this shiftless man jobs after decades of frustration, was at pains to emphasize the contrast between them, even when the effort was costly. "I avoided applying for disability although I really needed it after my accident," he said. Earlier in their lives the distinction had been less clear. "We shared a room growing up," Jim said, "and it made me want to get away from home. I thought, 'That could be me—I want to make sure it's never me.' There are things you don't want to know." That his difference from his brother is tenuous was one of them.

Normal siblings anxiously scan their feelings and behavior—and even their appearance—for signs of the repudiated other. "I'm always afraid," said Mimi Newhouse, whose borderline sister had ruined her Thanksgiving. "Do I have this in my package? Is this why I've never been in a long-term relationship?" The very qualities they dread sharing have a way of showing up, like the siblings themselves, at the worst possible moment. When the connection can no longer be denied, a person's equilibrium can be seriously disrupted.

Jane London regularly reassured herself that she had nothing in common with the peculiar sister who had thrown herself down the stairs and whom she had frantically and unsuccessfully tried to introduce to men. "I used to think one of us was adopted," she said. "We just don't belong in the same family." Like a mantra, Jane repeated, "We look nothing alike." She made sure that they acted nothing alike either. "It's scary to have a sister who's just not making it. I pushed myself socially and professionally because I want to see myself as healthy and not debilitated like her." When Jane's husband deserted her and their three children, however, the carefully nurtured distinctions seemed to vanish. "I wondered why my marriage didn't work. This was very subterranean, but I thought, 'Here we are, two sisters, and neither of us is married.'"

Since Jane had reported dreaming that her pregnancy had caused her sister to commit suicide, I asked whether the divorce had made her consider taking her own life. "I did take an overdose then," she admitted with shame. Why had she omitted mentioning this obvious resemblance until pressed? "I probably wanted to keep it separate," she answered. "I'm so afraid of being like her that I was blind to the connection. I keep looking for differences because I don't want to see similarities. I tell myself that I've got it together. It's like a curse on our family that I could end up as lonely, lost, and empty as she is."

Fear of contagion causes a person to overgeneralize, to confuse having a character trait in common with being identical to a sibling, as though any drop of the other's pathology polluted the entire personality. The context of Jane's despair was far more circumscribed than her sister's and its impact far less serious; Jane regained her resilience, but her sister had none to recover.

Repudiators believe that their health and sanity are precarious and contingent on having nothing in common with the damaged sibling. They assume that their problems are not really their own, that their doom is borrowed from an external source. The fear of contagion is a failure to differentiate; the sibling's flaws feel like a malignant magnet that can suck you in (one man called it a "gravitational pull") rather than an aspect of shared history and personality that must be negotiated.

It is realistic not to want to be too closely associated with a sibling who does not function; being able to distance oneself is part of being the normal one. But feeling horror and self-loathing at any shared characteristic indicates major unfinished business with the sibling and the self; to hate or fear the one is to hate or fear the other.

As a young child, Sharon Bergman was sexually molested by her deeply disturbed older sister. Although Sharon has had no contact with her tormentor for years, she still feels invaded by her. Even seemingly benign traits in common seem ominous. "If I ever see that my handwriting resembles hers or hear something similar in my voice, it gives me a tiny 'oh my God' feeling," she said. "She had a hand tremor, and sometimes my hands shake. I don't want to see that in myself. I picture myself as being so distinct from her, making such different choices." Sharon fears that all her efforts at differentiating herself are in vain, and what she sees makes her physically ill. "I'm practiced in being streamlined, in creating a nice, sleek shell, a sense of polish, but when my hand shakes, I think, 'This is a crack; nasty stuff might seep out.' At the edge of my brain I have a feeling that something in my core is damaged or stinking or repellent. I don't want to have any of her characteristics—it would mean I have some piece of me that's crazy like her."

Sharon still feels like her sister's victim. To free herself, she must recognize that the "nasty stuff"—her own perversity and her desire to exploit the helpless—is her own, no matter what the original source. She also needs to add the category "different but with things in common" to her emotional vocabulary.

Carrie Grainger is a lovely young woman with a glamorous career in the fashion industry, but she lives in terror that she will become schizophrenic—or that she already has the telltale signs. "I worry that somebody will turn me a certain way and spot my defect," she confessed. "For example, I'm shy on the phone, so I make it very quick. I'm seen as cold, but really I need to hang up so I don't screw up. It's not wanting to be found out." Carrie's adored brother, who was only a year younger than she and with whom she had shared a bedroom for twelve years, had a breakdown at seventeen from which he never recovered. She does not trust her reprieve. "I get heebed out if I'm not doing enough or I have quiet lazy days," she said. "I live in fear that like him I'll be fine, and then I'll get sick suddenly. There's a general feeling that things will fall apart any minute."

Carrie's emotional and physical closeness to her brother, as well as her guilt about distancing herself from him, exacerbate her fantasy that she must share his fate. Like many siblings of the mentally ill, she wonders whether she has really been spared and whether she deserves to be. "I didn't help him enough," she frets. "I went on with my life. I stopped missing him." Going mad herself would be a fitting punishment for repudiating him.

Boundaries with damaged siblings are disturbingly permeable. Their faces stare back at you from your mirror or from your child's face, and you see a nightmare version of your fate reflected in their ruined lives.

Jessica Kaplan's older sister Ricky had tenderly nurtured her when she was a baby, but envy later turned Ricky's love to hate. "I can't hold on to my good memories of my sister even though I have them because she turned on me so chillingly," Jessica said. "She terrifies me." It is not only the way Ricky treated her that chills Jessica; Ricky's treatment of her own child feels like a monstrous premonition. "She let her husband beat her daughter, and her son is a suicidal male prostitute. This is horrible—could I become as bad a mother as she? There are dangerous similarities between us. I could destroy my better life. Maybe that's why I want to stay away," she concluded. Understanding the purpose repudiation serves can diminish its power.

"I look at my sister Martha, and I see this total mirror of myself in her face, and I get embarrassed because I sound just like my sister Denise," said Ashley King, a dancer who is the only functioning member of her large and disreputable family. "It makes me feel so weird, like I've left my body. I get sick to my stomach. All I want to do is to show them that I'm not like them because they are such losers. It's difficult to realize they don't reflect who I am." Despite her siblings' visceral effect on her, Ashley struggles to disentangle her identity from theirs by talking rationally to herself and making efforts in her own behalf. "I'm such a hard worker—I take my profession very seriously," she said with justified pride. "I tell myself you can't choose your family, that I'm like them, but that I make different decisions."

Sibling contagion feels hereditary even if the disability is not congenital; believing oneself to be the bearer of bad genes is one form of repudiation. Diana Lamm is threatened by her brother's malign influence not only on her own sanity but on her son's. "When my son was born and people said he looked like Ron, it sent shivers down my spine," she said, as though her son were predestined to reproduce his uncle's life. Although Diana, a political speechwriter with a stable marriage and family, keeps her brother, a much-divorced alcoholic dentist accused of raping his patients, at arm's length, a creepy pronouncement of his reverberates in her brain. "He once told me, 'You're just like me—whatever I have, you have,'" she said. "So my every self-destructive streak or impulse makes me think, 'Am I playing out the family dynamic?' It haunts me." Her brother is trying to drag her down to his level by asserting a spurious identity between them, but Diana cannot see this because it jibes with her own worst fears.

Normal abnormal moments, the lapses of rationality that everybody experiences, are portentous for Diana as they are not for people without a sibling Mr. Hyde lurking in their psyche. "I'm so terrified of mental illness that I misinterpret the normal peaks and valleys people have. My husband doesn't feel it the way I do, it doesn't touch him," she said enviously. Hypervigilant normal siblings need to recognize the irrational origin of their fears for their children and themselves. It helps to have a mate who validates your sanity—even if he or she cannot empathize with your dread—and who neutralizes the malign influence of a brother's hateful wishes.

The greater the trauma, and the more successful the surviving sibling, the more she suffers from shame and fear of exposure. Barbara Green, the high-powered CEO of an advertising agency, had a wretched family history to hide. Her sister was severely retarded, and her older brother had committed suicide when she was a teenager. "My closets are so full," she commented. Her anxiety surfaced in a dream:

> I'm in Saks Fifth Ave, but I don't have my shoes on, and I don't want anybody to see. The floor is disgusting. I say to myself, "I'll just go and buy a pair"—but people will still know that I came in without them.

Even though she is now living a put-together life of Saks Fifth Avenue elegance and can afford to buy fancy shoes, there is no concealing that she came into the "store" barefoot. She can never effectively remove the evidence of her "filthy" past, the floor on which she walks. Covering up is not the answer for Barbara; she has to clean out her closets.

It is impossible to be fully aware of the power that repudiation exerts on your life choices; even women who make conscious efforts to remove themselves from pathological brothers end up inadvertently marrying men just like them.

Lawyer Pam Lewis, whose paranoid schizophrenic brother broke down her office door and gave her daughters the penis-shaped nutcracker, knew she was "attracted to the dark side" because of him. "I've always had friends who were mentally unbalanced or extremely weird," she admitted. Did the "bizarre man" she recently divorced remind her of her brother? Pam seemed taken aback at this question. "I always thought he resembled my crazy father, but gee, my husband's a lot like my brother, now that you mention it," she said. "I never made the connection."

I asked Lisa Masterson, the "genetically engineered caretaker" of her psychopathic, drug-addicted brother, if he reminded her of her psychopathic, drug-addicted former husband. She too "didn't connect" the two men. "I never saw any of James's tendencies because I have this heartbreaking problem with my brother John. I viewed him as more like me, somebody else who took care of everybody. He was my helpmate to help John. "Psychological thinking was never part of my world—awareness is so fabulously lacking in our society."

Although Lisa failed to see the similarity between her brother and her husband, she dwelled so anxiously on the potential similarity between her brother and any child of hers that she decided not to have any. "I'm deathly afraid to have a kid with a problem," she said.

Like Diana and many other normal siblings, she projected fears about sharing her brother's pathology onto the next generation.

REPUDIATION IS AN INTERNAL PSYCHOLOGICAL MANEUVER, a defense provoked by anxiety that the damage will infiltrate your personality. It is possible to repudiate a sibling you see every day, as I did. Estrangement and disengagement, in contrast, are the realistic responses of a normal sibling who recognizes that no healthy relationship with the damaged one is possible. Biology, even coupled with compassion and insight, may not be enough to sustain it.

Some siblings feel like changelings, beings from an alien universe. Their parents imagine that they took the wrong child home from the hospital. An unhappy combination of character traits, subtle disabilities of unknown origin, and family dynamics makes any common ground there ever was irretrievable; these siblings are too disturbed or too disturbing to have in your world. When efforts to reach them fail, normal ones are left with a void where a brother or sister ought to be.

"He has a different vocabulary for life" is the way Candace Peters describes her peculiar brother, who was one of those boys who relates more to electronic gadgets (and later to computers) than to people. "He never wanted to be part of the family," she said. "He was never there in the first place—he had nothing to do with our lifestyle. Everything about him was strange. I can't imagine it any other way. My mother says, 'I don't know where he came from—and you're just like me,' and my father tried to tolerate what he couldn't make sense of." Candace, a hard-driving investment banker, is "completely estranged" from this "shut-down, dyslexic oddball" who barely supports himself and continues to sow dissension, as he did when he was an assaultive, alienated child.

Candace "attempted to rectify" the family feud that her brother provoked years ago, but to no avail. "Every year I used to send him a birthday card telling him the news, which he never answered. He never acknowledged my daughter's birth." Now she is not indifferent to him, but she accepts that there can be no rapprochement. "Why would I go back to get something I'm never going to get?" she said. "My disconnection from him is so powerful that I've disconnected from it. I imagine it's all about pain. He doesn't have the means to work through his problems. I'm sad that he's paralyzed in his fear and that that is all he can do. I feel he isn't in my family anymore."

Candace was struck by how many women of her acquaintance have similar situations with their brothers. "In my investment group, everyone has a difficult brother, everyone is the biggest money maker in the family, and nobody talks about it," she observed. "Why is this so closed off?" Residual guilt, sorrow, and shame keep nonfunctioning siblings safely sealed away.

Maggie Payne, whose borderline sister has fought with her for decades, had a similar experience when she asked members of her book club to volunteer to be interviewed on this topic. "They all shrank back," she said, "and I know that several of them have brothers who are a disaster. Why is this so hard to discuss? You have to admit the isolation of it, that you are embarrassed and upset." Maggie herself understands this reaction from the inside. "Only people who know me extremely well know I have a sister; she's not part of my life." Until recently Maggie never mentioned her sister's name because "it would have made her too real." Although she wants nothing more to do with the woman with whom she "never remember[s] a happy moment," she spoke about their shattered relationship with obvious distress. "She's had a profound effect on every area of my life," she said. "I wish she would have tried to understand; I would have been receptive. I've worked so hard on it." Although it grieves Maggie that they never will have a happy moment together, speaking her sister's name aloud permits her to work through their relationship within herself.

"Five years into therapy my therapist asked me why I never called my sister by name," said Jacob Wilde. "I got defensive, but he was correct. She is the door that never gets opened." Jacob and his embittered, isolated sister have not spoken for fifteen years. "Even thinking about her, let alone making contact with her, unsettles my image of my self, my life, and my family," he said. "I have my crazy core too, my own place where I don't want to reach out or be bothered with anybody. I'm not so different. Even though I molded myself into her opposite, I recognize there is another half to me—the shadow me that is 'not her,' the self I'm not supposed to be." You can never integrate what you amputate, and nobody without a shadow is real.

identification

Repudiators flee their shadows; overidentified siblings are enveloped in theirs. While they too strive to be different, they fear they are doomed to fail. They think they share more pathology than they actually do because they are psychically merged with their damaged brother or sister.

Marilyn Daniels, whose brother murdered a policeman, practically feels she committed the crime herself because she and her brother share DNA. "Just because I got a few more IQ points doesn't mean I don't have the same tendency," insisted this kind, highly responsible woman, who felt so guilty that she dropped out of college to punish herself at the time. "He's big and strong like me. Part of me longs for constant stimulation just like him. We're so connected it's amazing—he got the matter, and I got the antimatter. I know I'm the kind of person who could kill. Put me in a dark room with a baseball bat, and you want to be on my team, not the opposition. If this hadn't happened to him, who knows what I would have done?"

Convinced that her brother's act was a monstrous reflection on her own character, Marilyn isolated herself for years afterward. "It became harder to connect," she said. "What would people think of me?" Although she is now more forgiving of herself—and has never committed an aggressive act—she still does not trust her ability to control her hostility. "I continually question myself. I have to be on point to be sure I'm doing things right, because my standards are really low." Physiological kinship blinds her to her moral superiority.

Gentle people fear that they could be violent, and lively ones worry that they are dull. Ellen O'Brian, the thoughtful and intensely emotional illustrator, imagines that she is as tedious and flat as her seriously learning-disabled sister. "My identification with her is huge," said Ellen. "She's like some part of me—the worst part. She talks in a monotone about boring details, so when I ramble, I get concerned. She's definitely the source of my insecurity—'Will people like me? Am I strange like her?'"

Ellen believes she is indelibly tarred with the same brush as her unappealing sister because she was "clumped with her" by parents who prevented her from expressing anger and by classmates who picked on them both. Even though she overstates the case, she correctly identifies one damaging attitude they have in common: "the forced cheerfulness that covers an icky, painful sense of being defective." Years of reflection have helped the high-functioning sister overcome this unwelcome evidence of kinship. "I broke out of my shyness, although I still worry that no one will want me," she says, "and I'm trying not to be cut off from feelings." Developing herself in ways her sister cannot is teaching her that to share tendencies with another is not to share destinies.

Identifying too closely with a mentally ill sibling can be hazardous to your health. Psychiatrist Laura Russo's manic-depressive younger brother Tom, whom she had always admired for his daring and independence, once took her for a walk over slippery boulders on an ocean jetty in a storm. "The waves were crashing over the rocks," she remembered, "and he kept trying to edge me out. He wouldn't have minded if one or both of us had gone under—and I thought I was chicken for not doing what he wanted."

Laura was so merged with her beloved brother—and so invested in denying Tom's insanity—that she saw herself as a coward rather than him as a would-be fratricide. "Here I am in the profession," she said, "and I refused to believe Tom was ill until later, when he tried to hijack an airplane. Then I was stunned that I'd been confusing destructiveness with strength. I'd idealized him; I needed a healthy member of the family."

Twenty years after this horrifying incident, the toll Tom's illness has taken is unmistakable. "He was like a terrified animal when he had the breakdown," said his stylish, artistic sister with quiet anguish. "Now he looks like a weird homeless man. He's stabilized on medication, but hollowed out; it's like he's not there—I can't find the brother I love." With guilt and grief-stricken relief, she sees how alien he has become: "To see that Tom's the one suffering so greatly is unfathomable. It's a place I don't understand or make sense of. On one hand there's torment, and on the other secret gratitude that it's not me, that I never had to go to that degree, that I could always pull myself out. I'm very adept at protecting myself, but I have a deep resonance with his agony."

Laura never forgets how much the sophisticated physician and the sedated madman have in common; in fact, she is so acutely aware of her own potential for psychosis that she blurs the distinction between them. "He came out of the womb worried, but I was terribly shy as a child and didn't have any fun in my soul," she told me. "You might just as easily have thought I would be the one to have problems. There's a genetic component to this, so there but for the grace of God go I. We share a depressive core. I've gotten off easy—I just got the core; he got the whole ball of wax. I identify with him as being lost in the world; I have visited the shell he can't crawl out of. I never feel I'm all that far away from it; none of us are. My wearing black is not a fashion statement."

Laura still admires her brother's will and denigrates her own. "I wouldn't have the courage that Tom has to go on because I know the torture he's been through—I would have suicided long ago." She also knows how she has restricted her life and what she has lost to ensure her sanity: "I think, as he does, that people are not comforting, so I didn't marry—to care so much and hate so much would have made me more vulnerable, and that's not unlike him. In some ways he is my twin brother."

Although she knew it would be helpful to her to discuss Tom

("naming a disability makes it real"), Laura dreaded it; she still sees the world too much from her brother's paranoid perspective. "I'm terrified he'll read this," she told me, "and recognize himself, that he'll see how I have exposed him. It would reinforce the fact that he does not deserve to live because he's so crazy. To diagnose him or talk about him, even anonymously, feels like a betrayal."

When Laura calls Tom's delusion that his madness deserves the death penalty a "fact," and discussing her own feelings about their relationship a "betrayal," she shows how much her identity is still fused with his. Mental illness is not a capital offense, and she should not forfeit the right to her professional or personal judgments. To consider them intentional humiliations is her projection.

Disentangling one's own identity from a once-intimate sibling's is a lifelong process that is never watertight. Nonetheless Laura no longer denies major ways in which her world diverges from Tom's. "His safest state is to have nothing asked of him," she said. "That's not me; I want a lot asked. I am astonished at how much I've shaken loose from the brother I so adored, and how much our connection was based on my not recognizing who he was."

The distance separating the normal sibling from the abnormal one may still not feel very great at moments, but it is the difference between a vibrant if poignant life and a living death. The metaphor Laura used for this difference unconsciously recalls the fateful moment on the jetty when she began to define the boundary between them by refusing to be edged out to madness and returning to the shore: "he slipped through the cracks."

chapter 12

The Caliban Syndrome II: Acknowledgment

COMING TO TERMS with Caliban means that the "thing of darkness"—now not so dark and not so much of a thing—feels fully "mine." In my case, and for many normal siblings, acknowledgment meant recognizing that I made my closest relative into a "thing," that his image was indeed a dark force in my life, and that I denied ownership of the intimate, indelible connection between us. Affirming this truth required me to grieve for the pain I inflicted and the pain I suffered. It forced me to see through my myth of the happy family and the fantasy that I escaped unscathed or blameless. I had to face every feeling, no matter how shocking: that I hated, envied, and despised my own brother and wanted to get rid of him; that I took pleasure in his damaged state and wanted to call attention to it to elevate my own status in my family; that I did not want him to get better; and that I enjoyed my special place and its privileges. It also meant recognizing that my own childhood was amputated and that I was deprived of a precious bond that sustains other siblings and enriches their lives.

Acknowledging and owning the Caliban within does not change reality; it changes perspective. Coming to terms with a relationship does not necessarily improve the relationship or, as I found to my sorrow, bring about a lasting reconciliation. It does, however, increase compassion for Caliban and for yourself.

Acknowledgment takes a lifetime. It begins with recognizing that there is something to acknowledge in the first place, and it consists of equal parts mourning and appreciating, forgiving (at least yourself) and allotting responsibility. Many people use the metaphor of reluctantly opening doors ("my sister is the door I never open"; "I'm afraid that if I open that door, I'll never be able to close it")—usually ones that have been heavily padlocked and then concealed. Calling your brother or sister by name, and no longer excluding them from your thoughts, is an indication that the process has begun. Memories may resurface. Powerful, unexpected new emotions emerge; when siblings have been erased, increased anxiety about them should be welcomed. You may find yourself not crying as much, or as in my case, the tears may start.

My relationship with my brother, which so closely mirrors Miranda's with Caliban in *The Tempest*, exemplified the Caliban Syndrome. Survivor guilt, the only symptom I ostensibly lacked, proved the most telling, and the key to lessening its hold on me.

The four symptoms of the Caliban Syndrome diminish as acknowledgment proceeds:

premature maturity

Premature maturity becomes maturity—usually manifested as increased tolerance for immaturity. People feel that their lives no longer depend on being the good, undemanding, unflinchingly responsible, or self-sufficient miniadults their parents needed them to be, which also allows them to allow their own children to be children.

survivor guilt

Gratitude for good fortune replaces self-blame that it is undeserved, and accomplishments can be celebrated free of concern that they harm siblings.

compulsion to achieve

Success is no longer seen as an urgent necessity to compensate parents; people learn to relax.

fear of contagion

Repudiation and identification give way to compassionate recognition of partial kinship.

*   *   *

IN MIDDLE AGE two women with different family dynamics have come to similar conclusions about their situations. Each has mature understanding and acceptance coupled with self-knowledge that illuminates how she has overcome the Caliban Syndrome.

Janice Becker, the screenwriter who endured the double nightmares of fishing her psychotic sister out of the river and losing her depressed brother to suicide, is philosophical about her experiences. "Maybe I'm just a superficial person," this amiable, considerate woman suggested lightly but not unseriously. "I was guilty for a while, but then I realized that's stupid—what's the point of feeling guilty for your health?"

Both tragedies affect Janice deeply. She is not above weeping when she describes either her sister's degradation or her brother's death, and she "always has flowers at church for his birthday," but she knows her sanity distances her from both of them forever, and she is grateful for it. "I used to feel terrible that I wasn't understanding enough, because I knew things affected them in ways they didn't affect me," she said. "I could never understand the depth of despair he felt or comprehend her self-destructiveness. You do things if you love the person, so how come I can't make the extra leap to concentrate? I can't do it, and thank God I can't. I have a happy fulfilling life by refusing to be an active participant in pathological family behavior. What separates us is, I know I'm not mentally ill; I'm part of them, but I'm not."

Janice has come to feel responsible only for her own efforts and achievements, not for accidents of fate. "Years ago I wondered, 'Why is it them and not me? What made the roll of the dice go one way for me?' Now I realize that that's the nature of dice." Despite a lifetime of trauma, no one is less a victim than she. "Nobody has a normal family; it's a sliding scale. It's up to you to make what you can of what you have. It takes work—and," she adds with a knowing laugh, "superficiality."

Nina Parsons' envious, fragile, perpetually unemployed sister causes her aggravation and distress rather than anguish, but she too has learned to count her blessings. "I've made a decision not to be bitter," says this thoughtful playwright who has to work as a drama teacher to make a living. "I understand depression from the inside, but I've always been able to edge myself out of it." One way she does this is to discharge her hostility through art: she wrote a play about an envious sister who kills herself. Like therapists and special educators, artists are overrepresented among normal siblings. Fear of contagion has dissipated over the years and turned to relief. Nina does not apologize for her advantages. "When a sister's deformed, you're afraid it's catching, but when you grow up, you realize you're fortunate. You appreciate your luck compared to the other's misfortune, but you don't gloat because you're a decent person. The juxtaposition of weakness makes you appreciate your strengths and take more risks." Nina has also accepted the limitations of her relationship with her sister and found more functional, more generous replacements. "I've substituted close relationships with friends," she said. "They're like my older sisters now."

Once the rage that so many suppress surfaces and diminishes, sorrow comes to the fore; to know what you have gained, you must face what you have lost. Therefore mourning for the past, for what one woman called "my lost childhood," is a critical step in the integration process and one that is often neglected. As Jackie Hanson said, "Once I dealt with my intense guilt and anger about her, next came mourning and sadness; I saw what holes there were in my life.

People say you can't miss something you never had, but I definitely feel I missed out." Normal ones grieve for the loss of their childhood, their innocence, their possibilities for a unique kind of companionship, and for a feeling of optimism and order in the world that may not be realistic but keeps most people going. Their sorrow is not only about the past but about a future that can never be. "I think of all the adult rituals that other siblings have," said Jackie, "and I suddenly realize somebody's absent. My sister will never help me plan my wedding. A random law of nature that went awry caused this; it makes no sense then and now."

Though the grief can seem unsupportable, it is the most authentic emotion many siblings feel and one that was too threatening to express growing up. "I always seem more connected to myself when I'm really, really sad," said Carrie Grainger, whose schizophrenic brother disappeared into a mental hospital when he was seventeen. Before she cut off her feelings radically to protect herself, she remembered missing him so much that she would lie on the floor in his room and smell the carpet to remind herself of him. "I saw a movie trailer about two siblings where one breaks down, and I left the theater," she told me. If Carrie follows her grief wherever it leads, which is possible now that she has maturity, experience, and support, she will be able to remain in the theater in the future and perhaps regain some of her tie with her beloved, doomed brother.

Candy Fine, who is so afraid of her brother's bizarre violence that she is moving to France, is also oppressed by the tragedy of his life. "My brother's situation gives me an underlying sense of sadness, particularly after he lost his memory, for reasons no doctor can explain," she said. "What is it all for? Why are people born to live in this prison? He's had such a lonely, misunderstood life; when he dies, it will be the end of his sentence." This grief may never completely leave her, but she needs to realize and accept—as shocking as it sounds—that his death will end her sentence too.

Since coping with an abnormal child consumes massive amounts of a family's energy, normal ones are forced to shortchange their own experiences and feelings. "There are large gaps in my childhood," said Manny Resnick, who forfeited his acceptance to medical school so his obsessive-compulsive brother could attend. "I have only the outlines. When you grow up in a household with this going on, you shove everything under the rug, so my memories are attenuated." One of the things that is lost is your natural place and even your gender role in the family hierarchy. "I had to be the big brother," said the sister who was five years younger than her retarded brother. Normal ones know that the tumult of healthy family life—confidences, squabbles, moments of solidarity—is forever alien. A woman who always felt alone and estranged from her troubled sister said, "I always think growing up with regular siblings seems so foreign—how could it be possible?"

While mourning is necessary so there will be an end to mourning, many siblings are stuck in relentless, self-punitive remorse that makes closure impossible. In contrast, those whose brothers and sisters are functional hardly even remember childhood spats. At age fifty Pam Lewis still berates herself that she dressed her brother, who later became a paranoid schizophrenic, as a girl when he was three, as though she contributed to his pathology thereby. "I felt so bad looking back," she said. Carrie Grainger is sick with regret about her response as a typically clueless teenager to her soon-to-be-psychotic brother: "On my brother's sixteenth birthday, he wasn't sick yet, but he wasn't okay either. I got really furious with him and demanded, 'What's wrong with you for not being with friends?' I made him cry. It was the saddest moment of my life." More consistent lack of sympathy or empathy—let alone feeling repulsed, cold, or ashamed—provokes even more damning internal indictments. "My one regret in life is how I failed as a sister, that I couldn't feel compassion for my own brother," said Rebecca Ashford. Randy Lane condemned himself as "dishonorable and unchristian" for calling his brother names in a fight. Demanding saintliness of oneself is a symptom of unresolved premature maturity, and coming to realize that these untoward reactions are natural, inevitable, and no reflection on one's moral character is an essential part of self-acceptance. Embracing the abnormal sibling always involves embracing the flawed self as well.

Compensations for being the normal one emerge as grief and emotional perfectionism recede. Sober appreciation of what you have gained at so great a cost helps you feel consoled and proud. This recognition differs from the saccharine and self-obliterating exhortation to "count your blessings" forced on many normal ones in childhood, because it is based on having enumerated your curses first.

Many women with damaged brothers create intact surrogates through close friendships with men, as I have always done. "I seek brothers," Rebecca Ashford observed, "I treasure my male friends"— and she effortlessly feels the compassion for them that she lacks for her biological brother. Cindy Fine has a delicious, teasing camaraderie with a male coworker, complete with the practical jokes and nonsexual tussling that she would have longed to share with her actual brother if he had been robust enough. "I look for the sort of person who can take it," she said. Those whose sisters never functioned delight in their "wonderful women friends." Finding replacement siblings reaffirms their ability to feel fraternal love and assuages their grief for what will never be possible with their actual relatives. Adult satisfactions lessen the brunt of childhood sacrifices.

Women like Rebecca who were forced to assume inordinate responsibility for an unmanageable sibling are relieved not only to choose relationships as adults but also to be able to leave them guiltlessly. "I have a second chance of doing it right with my friends," Rebecca said. "I'll always be the reliable one, but I can change who I'm doing it for and not waste my time; inappropriate neediness, and I'm out of there."

Most normal siblings have no illusions about the difficulties of their childhoods, but they know that they also have more understanding as a result. Their self-knowledge is often deeper, their sensitivity to suffering heightened, and their appreciation of the human condition more profound than people who have had easier lives. Being a murderer's sister cost Marilyn Daniels years of anguish, but, she says, "it helped me to understand and embrace my own darkness. I really comprehend violence, rage, and drug addiction; we humans are all alike and so alone." Jennifer Martin's brother, afflicted with fatal muscular dystrophy, beat her when they were children and went on to become a scholar and spokesman for his illness before it killed him. "There's no scenario I can imagine that I couldn't handle because I've faced the worst already," she said. Her fury at her brother's brutality and her sorrow for his agony are now tempered with "immeasurable pride that he discovered a way to make a difference—that this man who would never be kissed found hope and love through his work." Anger at her own suffering commingles with appreciation for the courage that both siblings eventually showed.

Actor Jack Morelli feels that his reclusive sister is the source of his quirky humor, as well as the empathic solidarity with outsiders that informs his work. "I notice outcasts," said Jack. "My eyes are open in the margins because of Margaret; she's one of them. My impulse to be an artist comes out of some damage of my own and also from my sensitivity to her state, from thinking about it and watching it consciously." Jack no longer simply recoils from Margaret's strange personality, because he sees it as part of himself and as not without virtues: "We both have eccentric senses of humor based on strange repetitions—I've turned it into a successful style."

Jack is touched by the power of his parents' devotion to Margaret, misguided as it is. He also marvels at his sister's ability to enjoy the simple pleasures that are all she will ever have. "It's miraculous that she's never depressed. She's so thrilled and excited about the smallest things, like the first warm day. Margaret is now a source of pride," he said with admiration, even tinged with envy.

ALTHOUGH THE ESSENTIAL WORK of acknowledgment is integrating the subjective image of Caliban within the self, reconciliation—or a least a changed relationship—with the actual sibling frequently follows. The damaged one does not have to be capable of participating for this to occur and need not even be alive. But on rare and fortunate occasions a genuine rapprochement takes place—sometimes initiated by the newly insightful abnormal sibling himself.

Ben Ramsey never forgave his older brother David, the chronically unemployed singer whom he had dreamed coached him through his own first concert, for encouraging their father to disown him and kick him out of the house. "He had carte blanche in the family. His attitude was that I got what I deserved because I was provocative, so I had nothing more to do with him," said Ben, still smarting at age fifty-eight. "He's always been like a shape or an unpleasant presence that I try to stay away from as much as I can. There are lots of closed doors."

Ben was not exactly enthusiastic ten years ago, when David contacted him. "He was turning fifty and said he was setting goals and wanted to try to resolve the problems between us," Ben recalled. The meetings began shakily, "with lots of old hurts" on both sides. "In one of our first dinners," Ben recalled, "I told him he talks at me and doesn't have conversations. 'You're so self-centered,' he answered, 'that I feel I'm disappearing when you start to talk.' I realized that that's exactly how I feel with him—I experience another voluble presence making me disappear; there's no room for our two egos. As we continued talking, I found we both imagined each other as our father. I identified with him completely."

To their mutual astonishment, once they started communicating and listening to one another as adults outside their authoritarian father's sphere of influence, they found far more common ground than either could have imagined. Ben saw that neither of them had been spared, that each was both damaged and intact. He also started to appreciate David's virtues and to notice similarities that his own outrage had obscured. "He's more like me than my other siblings," Ben said. "The others rewrite, but he doesn't deny or make nice about how awful our father was. I had imagined he had the same vices as my father, but in fact he's a very good father himself. His two children are wonderful kids, and they're thriving. I really thought they'd be all fucked up, and they're great. It became more and more clear that the worst of him came out in relating to me."

The brothers now meet twice a year. David's grasping, devious wife, whom Ben detests, is a greater impediment to increased intimacy than David himself. While unconditional fraternal love will always elude them, much has been repaired. "He and I get along pretty well now and have gained more time—we talk about things besides personal history. We've put a lot to rest, and I can see he's a kind person. He's interesting—I like him now." The door that seemed barricaded forever has opened for good, and behind it Ben found a human being more genuinely related to him than he dreamed.

Only his death permitted my patient Nancy Solomon to convert her repudiation of and resignation to her brother into acknowledgment. With pained empathy I had been hearing about Nancy's wayward younger brother Joseph for years—how she tried repeatedly to make contact with him only to be rebuffed, how every conversation was strained and subtly accusatory, how she was unable to comprehend his life as a mostly unemployed technician living with a desperate welfare mother while she herself had long held a responsible job. I knew about her efforts to reconnect him with their parents, who had always preferred her and her middle-class life—her one success on his behalf. She had told me about Joseph's wild and lonely boyhood and how he had later turned to addiction and petty crime. Although her own childhood was full of pain and fear, she had been the dutiful daughter and the gifted student and had tried to be her brother's advocate far more than I had been for mine. But Joseph's sudden death at age forty-five, and the self-directed brutality with which he declined to fight his illness, was still a ghastly shock: though suffering from peritonitis and in extreme pain—the physician who performed the autopsy told her he had never seen anyone choose to endure such agony—he had refused to go to the hospital and had stayed silently in bed until the end.

Nancy was virtually motionless and mute for the next three months. She was overwhelmed not so much by the loss of her brother as by the circumstances of his death and what they revealed about his life, her life, and their relationship. The only way she could comprehend him, or assuage her guilt, was to mimic his self-destructive behavior.

Then one day she announced that she had finally said Kaddish for Joseph. Intoning the Jewish prayer for the dead laid many con-flicting emotions to rest and allowed her to voice others that had previously been unspeakable. "I accept that he let himself die," she told me. "I so much understand what his despair felt like, because I've felt it too—the horrible longing and the floundering, the dread of falling into a black hole and being the black hole. You're the end-lessly needy, empty vessel, and you're really angry at the same time—an empty vessel full of anger. When it comes down to brass tacks, you're out there alone and there is nobody to help."

Nancy understood that neither she nor anyone else could reach her brother, because no relationship can be sustained unilaterally; despite their shared despair, their paths no longer intersected. "At a certain point I just couldn't try anymore," she admitted. "What did I have in common with this man? I was the good child, and he was the bad one. I was not the best of sisters. We were opposites, and we were set in opposition by our parents, so we couldn't have each other for support or be a united source of strength. My relationship with my parents is much easier without him."

Three things changed as a result of Nancy's admission: she accepted her parents' offer to transfer Joseph's inheritance to her, she made them dinner and served the dishes that the three of them preferred but had avoided at family occasions because her brother disliked them, and she married the man she had been afraid to commit to for five years. She chose life.

TALKING IS A FUNDAMENTAL FORM of self-expression. Learning to speak their minds, to voice taboo thoughts and feelings, is critical for normal ones, who are so often nonpersons in their families and strangers to themselves. But for Jackie Hanson, whose sister Joan— the one who ate her homework—was mute as well as autistic, learning to speak for herself changed her life. It also made a genuine if forever wordless relationship with her sister possible.

Jackie's childhood mission was to provide her sister with a mouthpiece, and she had to silence herself to accomplish it. "She didn't have a voice, so I became her voice," she explained. "I'd make up what she was saying; it was as if I were actually speaking for her." For her part, Joan performed the role of the nonverbal pseudoconfidante: "I confided in her, but not in a meaningful, two-way way." So much of Jackie's energy was "directed to tuning into Joan and being perfect" that she tuned herself out. She never "revealed"—or even entered—her own inner world.

In Jackie's consciousness and in everyone else's eyes, the sisters were fused physically as well as vocally. "We look a lot alike, so people joke that we're twins. So much of how I understood myself was in relation to her—I defined myself not as an individual but as a conjoined [i.e., Siamese] twin." But since Joan was "destructive and embarrassing—she looks so normal, though her behavior is so abnormal," Jackie made sure that her own behavior was always constructive and a source of pride. "I couldn't be aggressive in public," she said. "I was so restrained because she was so much the opposite."

Maintaining this artificial state of merger kept Jackie ignorant of the parts of herself that were disturbingly like her sister. By depositing all rage and impulsiveness safely in Joan, and by assuming the role of Joan's devoted spokeswoman, she could remain Miranda-like; she was selfless in both senses of the word.

Two dreams revealed Jackie's predicament and how she resolved it. In the first she told herself why she became Jackie/Joan despite the liabilities:

> The newest camper in my bunk at summer camp was a frail, deformed child who barely looked like a person. Nobody wanted anything to do with her because she had sharp bony spikes; if you touched her she'd break, but it would also be very painful. I decided I had to be connected with her—this was the only person I could relate to—so I picked her up. I felt instant rapport, intense love, and an immense sense of fulfillment and gratitude.

"The spikes were her illness," Jackie said, "but her fragility was an illusion. We had this intense nonverbal bond where everything that needed to be said was spoken through contact, like a mind-meld. Nobody else paid attention to us."

Jackie's interpretation of her dream expresses her insights into the meaning of her merger with her actual sister and explains why she perpetuated a bond that was actually bondage. But the dream has an additional level of symbolic significance: her dream-sister is also herself, the part of her that feels fragile and repulsive, that is harmful and frightening to others, that retreats into a wordless, infantile, symbiotic world with Joan. Their idealized blissful union allowed Jackie to avoid the real world, real relationships, and threatening feelings. But in the dream Jackie was telling herself that the spiky camper is also the she-Caliban within who must be acknowledged and distinguished if the real Jackie is to speak.

Jackie's second dream, which she had after her sister was institutionalized, indicated that the separation was proceeding. Although it fulfilled a lifelong fantasy, she felt sad when she awoke:

> People were being split up into groups, and Joan and I were assigned to separate groups. She suddenly became much smaller—I was my adult size and I was holding her like a child. The adult me (I was an adult and a child at the same time) agreed that it would be okay, that she should go with them. Then all of a sudden she said one sentence: "I want to stay with you."

Since this dream was Jackie's creation, she was responsible for all its events. She separated her sister from herself, and she also put her own wish into her sister's mouth. These contradictory dream-actions reveal how conflicted she is about being "grouped" with Joan. The sadness she felt was her sense of loss as she chose to grow up and away from Joan. Accepting that she wanted to "split" from her sister allowed her to see herself as an adult, for to stay merged would have doomed her to be a speechless, dependent child forever.

The distinction between them had now become unmistakable. "She's not my peer," Jackie said. "We've not developed the same. We've diverged—she's immature and always will be."

Jackie now faced another hurdle. Once she discovered her own voice and learned to listen to it, the things she heard were shocking; she had to revise her self-image to include the Joan-parts and the buried feelings. "I felt intense guilt and anger at her that I never knew were there before," she said. "I had never let myself recognize I hated her because I would have hated myself; now I can't stop experiencing it." Jackie wisely credits recognizing her negative emotions with transforming her merger with Joan into genuine sisterhood; she recently decided to become Joan's guardian. "It feels fine and voluntary," she said. "I used to define connection as obligation—dealing with all my feelings about her changed that. Because I can be ambivalent, because I'm not denying, I can really relate to her now." Jackie knows that her merger with Joan also allowed her to avoid her true peers, who could speak. "I have to face this void and not fill it artificially," she said.

Separating from Joan not only permitted Jackie's individuality to develop; it inspired her vocation as a professional advocate for the disabled who frequently speaks out on the plight of normal siblings. This career is not a reflexive continuation of her earlier merger but expresses the mature desire to better the lot of Joan and others like her, as well as sympathy for others like herself. She has achieved what every normal one must strive for: to speak in a voice that is genuine and truly your own.

When you fully acknowledge Caliban, you are no longer the normal one, the person who either repudiates or identifies with your damaged sibling more than you know; you are yourself.

bibliography

The following works most influenced my understanding of siblings, especially those with abnormal brothers and sisters.

FICTION

William Shakespeare, *The Tempest*

Tennessee Williams, *The Glass Menagerie*

PSYCHOANALYTIC BOOKS AND PAPERS

Virtually all psychoanalytic texts, including every one I consulted, refer to *The Standard Edition of the Complete Psychological Works of Sigmund Freud* (London: Hogarth Press, 1966). Of Freud's works, *The Interpretation of Dreams* had the most direct influence on *The Normal One*.

Abrams, Jules, and Florence Kaslow, "Learning Disability and Family Dynamics: A Mutual Interaction," *Journal of Clinical Child Psychology* (Spring 1976): 35–40.

Describes the impact of a particular and subtle disability on families from a psychodynamic perspective.

Agger, Eloise, "Psychoanalytic Perspectives on Sibling Relationships," *Psychoanalytic Inquiry* 8 (1983): 3–30.

A seminal paper calling attention to this neglected area of study.

Akhtar, Salman, and Selma Kramer, ed., *Brothers and Sisters: Developmental, Dynamic, and Technical Aspects of the Sibling Relationship* (Northvale, NJ: Jason Aronson, 1999).

> *This book, written for professional psychoanalysts, consists of eight papers. Rosemary Balsam's brilliant (and accessibly written) contribution, "Sisters and Their Disappointing Brothers" was a revelation of my own buried psychology. Harold Blum's discussion of Balsam's paper, "The Legacy of the Defective and Dead Sibling," was also useful. Other papers in this book that informed my thinking included Salman Akhtar and Selma Kramer's "Beyond the Parental Orbit: Brothers, Sisters, and Others" and Vamik Volkan's "Childhood Sibling Rivalry and Unconscious Womb Fantasies in Adults."*

Balsam, Rosemary, "On Being Good: The Internalized Sibling with Examples from Late Adolescent Analyses," *Psychoanalytic Inquiry* 8 (1988): 66–87.

> *Insightful and helpful in understanding my own sibling experience.*

Bank, Stephen, and Michael Kahn, *The Sibling Bond* (New York: Basic Books, 1982).

> *Chapter 9, "The Embroiled Family: 'Well' and 'Disturbed' Siblings," clarified my understanding of how families (including my own) assign roles to siblings, and how these roles become part of each sibling's identity.*

Bergmann, Thesi, and Sidney Wolfe, "Observations of the Reactions of Healthy Children to their Chronically Ill Siblings," *Bulletin of the Philadelphia Association of Psychoanalysis* 21(1971): 145–61.

> *One of the earliest psychoanalytic attempts to understand the experience of normal ones via case studies.*

Charles, Marilyn, "Sibling Mysteries: Enactments of Unconscious Fears and Fantasies," *Psychoanalytic Review* 86, no. 6 (1999): 877–900.

> *This recent article was instrumental in clarifying how their own unresolved traumas cause parents to pass Caliban on.*

Graham, Ian, "The Sibling Object and Its Transferences: Alternate Organizer of the Middle Field," *Psychoanalytic Inquiry* 8 (1988): 88–107.

This paper helps explain and remedy the neglect of siblings in the psychoanalytic literature.

Lidz, Theodore, Stephen Fleck, Yrjo Alanen, and Alice Cornelison, "Schizophrenic Patients and Their Siblings," *Psychiatry* 26 (1963): 1–18.

In a study based on one of the most extensive, in-depth studies of the families of schizophrenics, the authors specifically address how and why the siblings of catastrophically disturbed people escape mental illness.

Solnit, Albert, Ruth Eissler, and Peter Neubauer, eds., *The Psychoanalytic Study of the Child* 38 (New Haven: Yale University Press, 1983).

One section of this annual volume is devoted to "The Sibling Experience." Of the six papers therein, Alice Colonna and Lottie Newman's "The Psychoanalytic Literature on Siblings"—which revealed the astonishing paucity of information about them—was eye-opening. "Parents and Siblings: Their Mutual Influences" by Marianne Kris and Samuel Ritvo, and Janice Abarbanel's "The Revival of the Sibling Experience During the Mother's Second Pregnancy," provided valuable insights into the hidden aspects of family dynamics. Hansi Kennedy's "Growing Up with a Handicapped Sibling," in volume 40 (1985) of the same publication, includes case studies that specifically address the unconscious aspects of being a normal one.

Titelman, David, "Grief, Guilt and Identification in Siblings of Schizophrenic Individuals," *Bulletin of the Menninger Clinic* 55 (1991): 72–85.

Case studies of anguished normal ones, written with great empathy.

Volkan, Vamik, and Gabriele Ast, *Siblings in the Unconscious and Psychopathology* (Madison, CT: International Universities Press, 1997).

Waugaman, Richard, "On Patients' Disclosure of Parents' and Siblings' Names During Treatment," *Journal of the American Psychoanalytic Association* 38 (1990): 167–94.

This paper makes the important point that calling siblings by their names makes them real.

OTHER (NONPSYCHOANALYTIC)
PSYCHOLOGICAL PUBLICATIONS

Seligman, Martin, *The Family with a Handicapped Child: Understanding and Treatment* (New York: Grune and Stratton, 1983).

Dr. Seligman's paper "Siblings of Handicapped Persons" describes the inner world and family experience of normal ones and surveys extant studies.

Stoneman, Zolinda, and Phyllis Berman, eds., *The Effects of Mental Retardation, Disability and Illness on Sibling Relationships: Research Issues and Challenges* (Baltimore: Paul H. Brookes, 1993).

An overview of research methodologies and findings.

Vadasy, Patricia, Rebecca Fewell, Donald Meyer, and Greg Schell, "Siblings of Handicapped Children: A Developmental Perspective on Family Interactions," *Family Relations* 33 (1984): 155–67.

A survey of studies on the effect of seriously disabled children on families.

BOOKS FOR THE GENERAL READER

Featherstone, Helen, *A Difference in the Family: Living with a Disabled Child* (New York: Penguin, 1981).

A moving and insightful work written by a psychologist about her own experience; it also includes research findings.

index